When the Student Is Ready the Master Will Appear

Jean Luc Lafitte

PublishAmerica
Baltimore

© 2006 by Jean Luc Lafitte.
All rights reserved. No part of this book may be reproduced, stored in a retrieval system or transmitted in any form or by any means without the prior written permission of the publishers, except by a reviewer who may quote brief passages in a review to be printed in a newspaper, magazine or journal.

First printing

At the specific preference of the author, PublishAmerica allowed this work to remain exactly as the author intended, verbatim, without editorial input.

ISBN: 1-4241-1649-X
PUBLISHED BY PUBLISHAMERICA, LLLP
www.publishamerica.com
Baltimore

Printed in the United States of America

Acknowledgments

The following people have made this journey possible, and for this I will be eternally grateful.

My children, Emmanuelle, Paloma, and Izzy, and my loyal friends who never gave up on me, and were there through rain and shine.

Sharon, my rudder in the storm, and the lighthouse that guided me home.

Tarique   Eddy and Heather
Dermot   Pam and Ralph
Steve   Karen
Peter   Toby
Ally   Wendy
Squibby   Nick Lamb
Mary   Janey

And finally to my family, especially Sara and Brian, who were there in the darkness shining light.

Jenny
Danny
Chanti
Isabelle
Emmanuelle
Jean

Introduction

This is a story about a person who could be male or female, young or old, because it has no race, creed or colour. In fact, if you want, you could say this story is about you. If you have picked up this book and are reading it, then your journey has just begun. Make yourself comfortable and make sure you are wearing good shoes, because we might be travelling over some rocky ground and have to face some tough terrain.

It has been said that when the student is ready the master will appear. Now, I would not be so presumptuous to assume I am the master, but rather a guide. My name is not important but if you want, and if it helps, you can call me Alex, for Alex is both a masculine and a feminine name. However, for the purpose of this story I will be masculine. You can see me as fat, thin, short or tall, so take a moment to imagine me in your mind and this is how I shall appear to you.

Chapter One

The time and date didn't mean that much, but I knew that as sure as the ocean moves in and out something had happened to me, and that my life would never be the same. In fact, I had a feeling from a very young age that my life would be a little different from the norm. The missing part in this belief, however, was how future events would unfold to justify this feeling. The fact that waking up to find yourself naked in the middle of a forest, when in reality you remember being tucked up in a warm bed, is, to say the least, confusing and a bit out of the normal. Yet here I was, strangely enough, not the least bit scared, or maybe I was just so confused I wasn't thinking straight.

I can't tell you what I thought had happened, but suffice to say I was a little confused, so if you'll forgive me, "Aaaaaaaaaaaaaa," or a sound to that effect, echoed through the forest. "Shit, help, what the hell am I doing here in the middle of nowhere, naked, alone?" were also thoughts racing through my mind. So now feeling very cold I was hit by fear and panic. What happened to my nice warm bed? What was happening? An alien abduction? God, I hope not because I didn't believe in little green men, and I wasn't ready to believe in them now. Maybe I had been drunk and this was a sort of initiation process by my friends, who thought that the idea of getting me drunk, and stripping me naked and then dumping me in the middle of the woods might be somehow amusing. "Well, hey, guess what, not very funny."

I picked myself up off the ground; my skin was patterned by the bracken and pine needles I had been sleeping on. I started searching for my clothes in an attempt to cover my modesty, not that anyone was around to see it. I started walking, even though I had no idea in which direction I was heading. I did remember that south tended to be the direction that most of the branches grew towards. Thank God for the boy scouts, I knew that one day something of what I had remembered would come in handy.

After a while, and with very sore feet, I had to sit down and start to think a bit more logically about what I was going to do, because if I wasn't careful I would spend the day going in circles, and eventually going out of my mind.

It's a strange thing but when you lose control of your normal, comfortable point of reference, you can very quickly also lose your mind. I sat down, closed my eyes and tried to contain my emotions, but the harder I tried the more they welled up inside me, "Aaaaaaaaaaaaaaaaaaa, fuck, shit, help!" I hit a tree with my fist in a combination of anger, frustration and fear. "Shit that hurt!" My fist was throbbing, what was I doing? Now I also had a sore hand to contend with. So alone, naked and afraid I did something I had not done in a very long time, I actually fell to my knees and prayed. The last time I had prayed was as a kid, but as I grew up and saw how religion and war appeared to go hand in hand, so I decided to leave praying to the religious people. However, here I was on my knees praying. Now, if there were a God, I would not blame him for not answering me because, let's be honest, would you talk to a friend who had snubbed you for years? Then when they suddenly want something, they decide to talk to you.

"Look God, please, if you are there, if you really exist, can you answer me? Help me. I'm in a lot of trouble right now and I could really do with a helping hand."

I must have repeated this sentence a few times, at the same time as clenching my hands together and keeping my eyes shut.

"Yeah," that's what I thought, nothing. Exhausted and filled with despair I fell to the ground. Lying on my back I finally let go, my body was limp and relaxed as I lay there in silence, staring up at the sun passing through the canopy of trees above. The leaves were emerald green and shafts of light danced among the branches. I don't know how long I was there but, lost in confusion and a feeling of despair, I closed my eyes and listened to the wind blowing softly around me.

Chapter Two

"I am here."

"Oh, that's good," I replied.

"So how can I help you?"

What? Who? Hold on. I suddenly realized someone was talking to me. For a moment I had forgotten I was stark naked in the middle of nowhere. I jumped up to see who it was, but wherever they were they must have been hiding well because I couldn't see anyone.

"Hey, could you help me?" I shouted out loud hoping they would hear me.

"Sure."

Again I turned in the direction of the voice but I couldn't see anyone.

"Look, I'm not a weirdo. I don't normally go around naked getting lost in the middle of a forest. I promise I won't hurt you. All I want is some clothes and directions to civilization, please. I really could use some help."

"Yes, I know, you said that before."

It sounded like a woman's voice.

"Look, can you just show yourself? Come out into the open. I promise all I want is a ticket out of here."

"Really? Are you sure?"

The voice was louder now and coming from behind me. I swung around and finally she was there in front of me.

"Oh, thank God for that. Look, can you help? Can you tell me where I am?"

She wasn't looking at my face and suddenly I remembered that I was stark naked. I quickly put my hands between my legs to cover my modesty.

"I know this all appears a bit bizarre but, trust me, I really don't know what happened to my clothes."

"Yes, I can see that," she said. "Do you usually lose your clothes?"

"No, really I don't know what happened to them. All I know is that I woke up in this wood and I found myself naked and lost. Where the hell am I?"

"Don't you remember?"

She was standing with her back to the sun and there appeared to be a translucent aura around her, but I didn't really dwell on this as my mind was fixed on my present predicament. Her dark, black hair cascaded around her face. A lock of her hair hung over one eye, which meant she had to look up. This made her gaze appear intense as her dark, brown eyes felt as though they were penetrating the depths my soul. Her skin was light brown and she reminded me of a painting I had seen once, by an artist called Russell Flint. I thought she might be Spanish or Native American Indian. Wherever she was from she was beautiful and this only made me feel more self-conscious.

"No, I don't remember. That's what I keep saying."

I felt like I was going in circles with this.

"Look, I know this looks really weird but, trust me, this is not normal and I don't make a habit of this."

"Listen," she said. "It's not much but I have a blanket in my cabin and I'm sure I can sort some clothes out for you."

"That sounds great. I really appreciate your help."

She turned and motioned for me to follow and I had the impression she was gliding on air; it's amazing what your mind does when it's stressed. Hopping around like a cat on a hot tin roof, and treading on pine needles and sharp twigs, I clenched my teeth in an attempt not to shout out loud and sound like a wimp. I awkwardly followed her. I had a feeling as if I knew her or we had met before, but I knew that this was impossible so I quickly put it out of my mind and concentrated on where I was going.

After some time we came across a log cabin, the sort that you see in the old westerns. I only say this because I was a fan of cowboy movies and they always had log cabins in them, you know the scene when the bad guys are hiding out from the law. There was even smoke coming out of the stone chimney and a horse tied up to a hitching post. She told me to stay where I was as she disappeared inside, appearing a few minutes later with a pair of jeans, a blanket, and a T-shirt. She turned her back as I changed and for the first time I started to feel more comfortable.

Chapter Three

"Would you like a coffee?" she asked.
"You don't know how good that sounds, that would be great."
"Do you want sugar?"
"I'm willing to take whatever's going. I'm just grateful you found me."
"I have to warn you, though, I make it strong."
"To be honest, I think that's what I need. It might help me to focus on how I got here."
As I sat outside and looked around, taking in my surroundings for the first time without the feeling of dread and hopelessness in my heart, I began to notice how beautiful it was. I had always loved the woods and had never felt comfortable in big cities, which was strange because before she had found me I was starting to get stressed out. It also dawned on me that I didn't know her name.
"Sorry," I shouted into the cabin, "I must appear really ignorant and ill-mannered but I don't even know your name."
"Noisulli. You pronounce it No-is-ulli," she said in a soft voice as she stood behind me with two cups of hot coffee in her hands.
"Oh, sorry, I didn't mean to shout."
"It's OK. This must be all a bit strange to you. So you say you have no idea how you got here?"
"Yeah, I just woke up and, well, the rest you know."
"Are the jeans OK?"
"Yes, great thanks. In fact, if I didn't know better, I would say they are a perfect fit." I suddenly realized that I hadn't even told my saviour who I was.
"My name is Alex by the way."

WHEN THE STUDENT IS READY THE MASTER WILL APPEAR

"Yes, I know," she said. "Pleased to meet you, Mr Alex," she replied with a little, gentle smile and nod of her head, which suggested she found this amusing.

In all the confusion I must have introduced myself, more than likely when I was stark naked. I felt my cheeks flush with embarrassment as I imagined what she must have thought, finding a naked man in the middle of the woods. To her credit she didn't run away but, then again, did that make her sane or crazy?

"Alex."

"Sorry, I was daydreaming. So, Noisulli, that's an unusual name. Is it Asian?"

"Not sure. It might be. It also may be due to the fact that my parents loved the hippy love and peace era."

Now it was my turn to smile. "Is it possible to use your phone? There are a few people I would like to call or, maybe, to be more precise, have a go at for getting me into this predicament."

"Sorry, I would love to help you, Alex, but I don't have one."

"Not even a mobile phone?"

"Not even a mobile. I like the peace and quiet and I find phones a bit of an intrusion."

"So what about the nearest town?"

"About a day or so away."

"You are joking, right?"

"No, really, and that's if you walk at an even pace. Mind you, it's half the distance if you go by horse."

"Well, if I could ride that may be an option, but as rule animals and I have a difference of opinion as to what constitutes a good working relationship. I once rode a horse as a child. The problem was I wanted to go right but the horse figured that left through the thorn bush was the best way. So we parted company and that was the beginning and end of my relationship with horses."

"Well, it looks like a long walk or, if you want, you can ride up behind me."

"Put like that, it looks like I don't have an option."

"There are always options, Alex. It's just a matter of choice."

I couldn't really argue the point on this one and, anyway, I didn't really have the energy so Noisulli suggested we head off in the morning as the day was drawing in and she said the horse got jumpy if he travelled at night.

It was only at this point that I realized how tired I felt, and I figured, in part, this must be due to running on adrenalin and the need to survive out of pure animal instinct and confusion.

Chapter Four

For the first time, she took me into the cabin, which was surprisingly sparse. There appeared to be the very basic essentials, a wood burning stove, a couple of camp beds and a table with three chairs. There was no running water that I could see and the light was provided by an oil-burning lamp.

"So what do you do when you come out here in the middle of nowhere?" I realized that I was asking a lot of questions and must have sounded pretty ungrateful, but curiosity got the better of me.

"Sorry, forget that, I didn't mean to be rude," I said.

"No problem, you must be hungry. Would you like something to eat?"

"To be honest, my stomach feels like my throat has been cut and I will take whatever is on offer."

"Well, horse is not on the menu, but I am sure I can rustle up something to satisfy your stomach." We both looked at each other and laughed. Her face was radiant and when she smiled it was as if her eyes shone and pierced the dim light of the cabin.

We laughed again and I started to feel more relaxed, as if Noisulli was less of a stranger now. I had only just met her but we talked with the ease of friends who had known each other for years.

Noisulli pointed me in the direction of a bowl of water and a towel. The cool water on my face felt good, and I closed my eyes, taking a deep breath and letting it out as I stood there with my face in my hands, just happy to be still and feel the drops of water run down my face. Everything appeared to be more intense, even the soft texture and smell of the face towel. I washed the dirt from my face and hands as the smell of the food being cooked made my stomach gurgle with delight and anticipation at the possibility of being nourished. It was not long before Noisulli gestured to me to take a seat, as she placed two bowls on the table. The food was a simple meal of soup and bread but it was the best soup and bread I had ever had. Maybe it was the way she cooked it or maybe I was just so hungry that anything would have tasted good.

We didn't talk much as we ate but now and then we would make awkward eye contact and I had a sense that she was still trying to figure me out and, to be honest, I was also trying to figure her out. Here was this beautiful woman in the middle of nowhere, content with her own company, who had plucked me from the middle of the woods and had offered me food and shelter. I knew nothing about her and yet that was unimportant.

I was so hungry that it didn't take long for me to finish eating.

"That was great, thank you."

"My pleasure. I have put a blanket on the camp bed for you. If you get cold in the night there is another one under the bed."

We said goodnight and I lay down on the bed feeling nourished and tired.

"Sleep well, Alex," she said.

"You, too, and thank you."

It wasn't long before I was drifting off to sleep.

Chapter Five

The light was blinding, or was it? All I knew was that I felt an immense peace and love and the sensation of being very light.
"Don't be afraid," he said. "All you have to do is remember and all will become clear."
"What will become clear?" I said. "Just tell me."
"Wake up, Alex. We had better get going before it gets too hot."
I slowly opened my eyes and there she was in front of me, this woman who I had only known for a few hours, like a vision before me with a hot cup of coffee, and a voice that could lull the angels to sleep.
I squinted as the morning light hit my eyes and the smell of the coffee shook me from my dream.
"Did you sleep well?" she said.
"Yes, in fact, I had such a strange dream."
"Not about eating horses I hope."
"No," I said. "I think that phase in my life has passed. No, it was about this…" I suddenly stopped. "Sorry, I don't really know you, and I am sure you don't want to listen to me rabbit on first thing in the morning about some weird dream I had."
"Listen, believe me, you come up as normal in the grand scheme of things when I think about some people I know. At least you are able to express yourself."
"OK. So there was this being."
"Oh," she said before I could finish, "the light being."
"Now that is weird. How did you know?" Beautiful and mysterious, this woman intrigued me more and more.
"This wood is ancient. My grandfather used to tell me stories as a child about the light beings or spirits of the wood that live here.

They come to us in dream time, usually at times of great change in our lives."

"Does being naked in the middle of the woods, not knowing how you got there, constitute great change? Because I can't think what they would want with me. I am just an ordinary Joe Bloggs."

"Don't you mean an extraordinary Alex? Who else do you know who can say they woke up naked in the woods and don't know how they got there?"

"Fair point, so extraordinary Alex it is, but that still does not answer the question as to how and why I am here."

"Ah, therein lies the mystery and the answer. In time you will remember and all will become clear."

Not her as well. That's what the light being said just before Noisulli woke me. I didn't say anything and decided that the events of the day before would most probably have convinced her I had lost the plot and maybe my mind. As far as I knew she might have slept all night with one eye open, in case this madman she had welcomed into her cabin turned out to be a convict on the run, and the reason he had no clothes was he had dumped his prison issue uniform in the vain hope of making his escape easier.

We finished our coffee and Noisulli saddled the horse. I looked at the beast of burden with some trepidation, as that memory from my past once again presented itself to that part of my brain that said "man walk and horse run," but I had no time to let the fear well up inside and churn it over like a piece of indigestible fat. The loan ranger was ready and she expected her Tonto to jump up behind her shouting "high ho silver away." Tonto, in this case, wanted to away but in the other direction.

"Come on, Alex, you have to face that fear at some time. It might as well be now. What are you, man or mouse?"

Now with a woman, especially a beautiful one who rescues you and then plays the fragile male ego card, you know there is only one thing you can do. "Squeak," was my reply and I mounted in a rather ungainly fashion.

"Hold tight," she said, so I grabbed the back of the saddle.

WHEN THE STUDENT IS READY THE MASTER WILL APPEAR

"No, silly, come here." Noisulli grabbed my arms and put them around her waist. I felt like a teenager on my first date. I'm sure I blushed; my heart was pounding in my chest. I was just glad that she couldn't see my face. I remember riding behind someone only once before in my life, but it was as a child in Africa being taken to kindergarten by my mother on the back of her bicycle. This was different, though. I was now a grown man, but the way I was feeling I might as well have been a boy.

The movement of the horse was quite sensual. I knew that I needed to take my mind somewhere else or this journey was going to be uncomfortable. I started thinking of that time on the back of my mother's bike as a child. Strange how in one's life there are certain memories that don't appear to have any meaning, yet stay with us with such clarity, often triggered time and time again by something as obscure as a sound or a smell. For me, it was usually when I saw a snake, which wasn't that often, but nonetheless it brought back the memory. The reason why it was a snake is as vivid as the memory itself. On that sunny morning on the way to the kindergarten we came across a dead snake on the road. It looked as though it had been run over by a car, and as we passed around it time appeared to slow. I remember staring at the snake. I noticed how beautiful its colour was, even in death. I pulled away from my thoughts of the past, as a leaf on a branch brushed across my face. This time the memory it triggered was when the horse and I parted company. Without realizing, I had grabbed Noisulli tighter. She didn't appear to be uncomfortable with this. Nonetheless, I loosened my hold and hoped I had not embarrassed her. The leaves in the canopy above painted shadow pictures on the ground, as small insects darted through them. My heart was at peace, and I couldn't tell you why, but I was content even though I still had no idea of how and why I came to be here.

Chapter Six

The morning drifted into afternoon without any more unexpected surprises, but by the time we stopped to rest the horse, my backside was grateful for the rest. Now I knew why John Wayne walked like he did. It wasn't because he was a tough cowboy, but more than likely he was suffering from being saddle sore.

Noisulli, on the other hand, dismounted as though she was as light as a feather, walking with the poise and grace of a ballet dancer. For all that I knew she may even have been a dancer.

"So what do you do when you aren't being a cowgirl and rescuing strangers from the woods?"

"Oh, this and that."

"Oh, this and that. Is that more of this or more of that?"

"This, usually."

She really wasn't going to give me much information, but then, to be fair, she knew nothing about me. I was fascinated by her, but she didn't appear to be that fussed in knowing about me.

"If I was to guess, I would say you must be a dancer or an artist." If in doubt go fishing, I thought to myself.

"No, I'm a teacher."

"I imagine you're a good one, you have a peaceful nature about you and children respond to that. Do you teach young or older children?"

"All ages, really. I step in when I'm needed.

"Alex, could you get some water for the horse? If you follow this path down the slope you come to a stream. The water is fresh and cool there."

"Sure, no problem."

WHEN THE STUDENT IS READY THE MASTER WILL APPEAR

She handed me a leather bag for the water. I made my way to the stream following her directions. The path was a bit narrow and the ground underfoot a bit slippery, so I made sure each step counted before taking the next one. The temperature started to change and it felt noticeably cooler; it also became darker as the surrounding trees and vegetation grew thicker. I could hear the stream in the distance so I knew I was going in the right direction. I shivered as the hair stood up on the back of my neck, like the sensation you get when someone has just walked over your grave.

There was no apparent reason but I was slightly uncomfortable. I guessed it could have been the unfamiliar surroundings and the change in temperature. I carried on towards the sound of running water. Eventually, I came into a clearing and found the stream.

There was a large tree that had fallen across part of the stream, forming a makeshift bridge. I decided to perch on it to reach the water. I leaned forward and lowered the bag into the stream, at the same time grabbing onto a branch to stop myself falling in.

Sitting there for a while as the bag filled with water, I took in my surroundings. The air was damp and the smell of wet soil permeated the forest. After daydreaming for a time, I turned to see if the bag was full and, in the reflection of the water, I caught sight of what looked like a woman, except she, or it, was what I could only describe as an angel or a being made from light. In complete shock I quickly turned to look over my shoulder and at the same time lost my footing and fell like a sack of potatoes backwards into the cold water. Coughing and spluttering and slightly winded I looked up but no one was there. What the hell was that? This just had to be the weirdest time of my life. To top it all, now I was hallucinating.

I climbed out of the river like a spider trying in vain to get out of the bath and managed to slip, this time landing face down in the stream. "Aaaaa, shit," I felt like exploding, which is what kind of happened next, as what felt like a surge of energy went through my whole body. I went rigid as I was lifted at least a foot into the air and then landed on the ground with a thud. I was in pain, my ribs felt bruised.

I crossed my arms across my chest and swore in frustration and anger.

"Alex, are you OK?"

It was Noisulli, and as I opened my eyes she was leaning over me with a look of concern on her face.

"Are you OK? What happened?"

"I'm fine, I just slipped."

"Are you sure? You don't look fine."

I had no intention of telling her I had just seen a being of light. Seeing me naked and now telling her I was hallucinating was really going to put the icing on the cake and make her think I was crazy.

If I was her, I would have mounted my trusty steed and bolted out of there, like a bullet from a gun.

"No, really, I'm OK. You know me. Anything to get your attention so you can save me again," I said laughingly.

She grabbed me under one arm and helped me to my feet. "Well, next time, just ask. You don't have to throw yourself into the water to get my attention."

"OK, I'll try to remember that."

I stood up, but straight away fell to the ground as the pain in my chest caused me to double up in agony.

"Alex, my God, what's wrong?"

"It's my ribs. I think I might have broken them."

I didn't know what a broken rib felt like but I knew I was in pain and I knew I wasn't just winded.

"Stay still. Don't try to move."

Noisulli ran off back down the path and returned riding the horse.

"OK. Do you think you can stand? I need to get you onto the horse."

I could see she was worried, so I gritted my teeth and tried to smile through the pain.

"Yes, I think I can do it. I just need to take it slow."

I don't know how but between us we managed to haul me up onto the horse. I sat slumped slightly forward as Noisulli climbed up behind me.

"Alex, I am going to hold onto you. I'll go as quick as we can; just tell me to stop if it's too painful."
"Don't worry, I will." The amount of pain I was in, I wasn't going to need any prompting.
Noisulli was really going to be glad she had met me, I thought ironically. So far I was trouble with a capital T. She rode the horse as fast and as carefully as she possibly could. Each bump caused me to tense my whole body, and take in a sharp breath.
"Where are we going?" I asked.
"Don't worry about that, just try and relax. I know someone who can help."
"I thought you said the closest town was a day's ride away."
Noisulli didn't answer, or she might have, it didn't really make a difference because at that point I passed out.

Chapter Seven

My body felt light as though it was floating in water, except there was no need for me to kick my feet or move my arms to stay afloat. Slowly I opened my eyes. I felt like a child lying on the grass in summer staring up at the sky, without a care in the world, seeing if I could make out shapes in the clouds. The sweet smell of wild flowers was carried on the breeze, as it gently blew against my face. In that moment I lost all perspective of where I was, and what was happening to me. It took some time for me to realize, but then it dawned on me that I was no longer in pain.

I had a sense that I wasn't alone, so I sat up slowly expecting to see Noisulli next to me, but she wasn't there. Then, and don't ask me why, I started to examine my limbs. First, counting my fingers to make sure they were all there. "Six," "seven," "eight," "nine," "ten," OK. All digits present.

"So have you remembered yet who you are?" came the voice.

I was still disorientated and I felt my self drifting in and out of consciousness or, at least, I think that's what happened. How else would this make any sense?

"So you still don't get it. Don't worry, the rest are just like you at first, a bit confused, but slowly and surely you begin to understand."

"Hold on, am I awake or am I dreaming? And who the hell are you?"

He was sitting there on the edge of the cliff looking off into the distance. The view was breathtaking and, if I didn't know better, I would say this was the Grand Canyon. I knew that was impossible, though. How did I get up here? There was no way I could have climbed up here in my present state and, whoever he was, he would have had to had superhuman strength to carry my body up this high on his own. Oh,

WHEN THE STUDENT IS READY THE MASTER WILL APPEAR

I get it, this is a dream. I closed my eyes but when I opened them again he was still there staring off into the distance. I was getting angry again, but at the same time very scared. First, I was naked in the woods, and then I met a woman who gave me a hard-on, and now this.

"Beautiful view is it not?" he said glibly, like this was a Sunday picnic.

He appeared to have no concept of my feelings, as if this was the most natural thing in the world to him, to be sitting here balanced on an outcrop of rock with a complete stranger.

"But I am not a stranger, Alex. Have you forgotten me already?"

"Look, buddy, you might think I know you, but I don't, and I could really do with someone giving me a straight answer, without all the bullshit that's designed to fuck my head up. Hold on, how did you know what I was thinking?"

"You know, when you were a boy you never swore. Not that I mind you swearing, you are a grown man now, but I didn't think you would do it in front of me."

What the hell was the mixed-up idiot talking about? Then he took his hood off and turned to face me. The first thing I noticed was his steel blue-grey eyes, and suddenly I recognised him. I backed up so fast I almost fell off the cliff.

"But, but," I blubbered in an attempt to make sense of what I was seeing. "You are dead. How's this possible?"

As a child, my grandfather used to take me fishing. I would try and catch the minnows in the rock pools, while he sat on the riverbank smoking his pipe. He was a man who didn't really say much, but in his silence I remembered a strength that needed no words or posture to define him. I have seldom met men like that since, and it is a quality I have always admired and tried to aspire to, only to find that, unfortunately, it's usually a quality you are born with.

"Are you really my grandfather? Am I dead? Is this heaven?"

"Now, which one of those questions do you want the answer to first?"

"All of them."

"So are you ready?" he said, not answering any of the questions.

"Hold on, do I get an answer?"

"Why give an answer to a person when they already know the answer? So if you are ready, shall we go?"

"Excuse me, ready for what?"

"To begin what you came here to do."

"Sorry, can we back up a bit? Did I miss something? You have to forgive me. First, I was naked in the woods, then there was a beautiful girl, broken ribs, which by the way strangely no longer hurt, and somewhere along the way I missed the part where you tell me what the hell is going on."

Then I lost it, something I was doing a lot of lately, but could you blame me?

"What the hell is going on? Are you trying to drive me nuts? Don't you think this joke has gone a bit too far? And do you want to know something? I don't think it's funny, and here is the latest newsflash, how about I rip your head off and we have a laugh about that?"

Did he react? Did he do anything? No, he just sat there, which is what my grandfather would have done, and then said, "That's it son, better out than in."

I sat down, took in a big breath and stared into the ground not really caring what happened. I no longer had the energy to fight anymore.

"So all done," he said.

"Sure, whatever you say."

I was a sheep ready to do whatever the wolf said. Just make it painless and quick, I thought.

"That's not a bad analogy," he said, "except you are not so much a sheep as a lamb, a big lamb, but none the less a lamb. So are you ready?" Again, he had been able to read my thoughts.

"Am I ready to shop, clean my teeth, jump up and down on the spot? No I am not ready. I would like to wake up and end this nightmare, be normal with normal people."

"OK. Shall we go?"

Nothing I was saying was getting through to him. Why, and I will never know why, but like the obedient sheep, or was it lamb? I followed him.

Chapter Eight

"So tell me, Alex, where do you think you are?"
"I don't know. Give me a clue."
"OK, I like games. A bit like life don't you think? Well, you are closer to being who you are than ever before."
"Does that mean I am not who I think I am?"
"Yes, good, that's about it."
"So who do you think I am?"
"Now that would spoil all the fun."

I didn't have time to reply because I started sinking into the ground. I looked down in absolute confusion, and saw the earth below me had turned to quicksand. It was pulling me under as if it had come alive, and I started to panic. Frantically, I looked around for something to hold onto.

"Hey, don't just stand there. Can't you see what's happening? Pull me out!"

He just stood there, like this was the most normal thing in the world, without an ounce of compassion that my life was in danger.

"Oh yes, quicksand. Strange you all get caught by that one, it amazes me you never see it."

"Are you going to help me?"

I was sinking fast and the thought of being killed by suffocation was creating an even greater panic in me. I started to struggle in an effort to save my life. I reached out my hand expecting him to grab hold of it. I was shouting at him to help me. I was up to my chest in quicksand and sinking deeper. I stretched out my hand again, but he just crouched down and sat there watching me, like a spider watching a helpless fly in a web.

"Stop struggling, Alex. Let go. All your life you have struggled and where did it get you? Did all those times worrying about tomorrow and the guilt of the past accomplish anything? I don't think so. Just give in and let go."

This was really twisted. My grandfather, or someone that looked like him, a man I loved and respected, just sat there offering no help.

My grandfather, if he were my grandfather, would never have done such a thing, and so in that moment I knew that this could not be my grandfather.

"Alex, remember when you were a child trying to catch those minnows? You jumped about splashing this way and that but whatever you did they were just too fast. What did I tell you to do?"

Great, a philosophical debate as I struggled to save my life.

"What did you do, Alex? Quick, think! You are sinking deeper."

"OK, not that it will save my life. You said let the fish come to you, relax, don't fight them."

"Then what happened?"

"Look, any chance of having this conversation after you save my life?"

"No."

"I caught one. Now can you get me out of here?"

Just before my head was about to go under, a wave of euphoria came over me. Somehow I found the strength to give up, and at that point I began floating to the surface. I closed my eyes, and when I opened them again I was lying on solid ground. I couldn't understand it, the ground was hard, and so I stood up and stamped on it just to make sure.

"Careful," he said. "You might make a hole in the ground."

I jumped away from the spot I was standing on, thinking it might turn into quicksand again. Then he laughed at me.

"Glad you think it's funny. This might be normal for you, but in case you didn't notice, a moment ago I was up to my neck in quicksand."

"Come on, follow me," he said, still with a smile on his face, totally ignoring my ranting and raving. So we walked on in silence, with me having no idea where I was going.

Chapter Nine

Sometime later the silence was broken, on my part, out of curiosity.

"So I know you look like my grandfather, but are you really him? I'm sure you aren't, but I just need to hear it from you."

"We are what you want us to be, Alex, but we find that you are more comfortable and less startled with someone who is more familiar to you."

"So what do I call you, if you're not my grandfather?"

"I am called many things. Sometimes a saint, and sometimes a sinner, but man has never really called me by my name. And yet with those you despise and call your enemy, you have no problem calling them by their name."

"Are you saying you are God?"

"Do you think I am God, Alex?"

"Well, I don't see a halo or long, white beard, and I don't remember in Sunday school being told anything about God letting people sink in quicksand. So, no, I don't think you are God. Mixed up and a bit weird, even eccentric, perhaps, but not God. Since I don't know your name, which I'm sure must be unpronounceable, do you mind if I call you Sam?"

"If you want. But why Sam?"

"Because I feel uncomfortable calling you grandfather, and I once had a good childhood friend called Sam."

"OK, Sam it is. I like the sound of that, and if it makes it easier for you go ahead. After all, I have been called worse."

Now that I was calmer, I broached the subject of the quicksand again.

"So Sam, tell me, what was all that quicksand business back there? Did you hypnotise me or something?"

"Yes, something."

"Oh right, a magician never gives his secrets away. I get it, don't worry, I also have a few secrets."

"Yes, I know, and your greatest secret is so secret you don't even know it what it is."

"And what is that meant to mean?" A bit like fungus, this guy was beginning to grow on me. His wit was sharp, and his sarcasm, though clever, never felt malicious.

"You're special and gifted and, though you don't know it yet, your pain comes from denying it."

"Are you hitting on me? Is this a gay kind of thing? If you are, but you think I might get weird on you, it's OK, don't worry, but just to let you know, I'm straight like an arrow and I only go one way."

"No, Alex," he said now, laughing. "I'm not gay, and that's why I'm so fond of you, because you know how to make me laugh. Do you know that's a gift in itself?"

"Yeah, well, that's good because laughter is good, and I knew you weren't gay, you know that, right?"

"You really thought I was gay?"

Now he was crying with laughter and, among all the weirdness, I did something I hadn't done since all this started, I also began to laugh. Not just a little laugh but the kind you did as a kid when your guts ached and you just couldn't stop even if you wanted to.

When we finally stopped laughing it felt good, like all the tension had been let go.

"Hell, I should do this more often." It was like I had forgotten how to play. I was so caught up with life, bills and work, I had lost the reason for living. In fact, I was just existing. I remember as a child having such great ideas about how I wanted to save the world. But that felt like such a long time ago, and somewhere in all the confusion I had lost the most important thing. This made me feel sad, and I felt the emotional pain rising up in my chest, as laughter turned to tears.

Here I was, a full-grown man, crying like a baby, and I didn't care.

WHEN THE STUDENT IS READY THE MASTER WILL APPEAR

Sam just sat there without saying a word, but when I finally wiped the tears from my eyes and told my self how silly I was being, he just looked at me with such compassion that I knew he understood.

He didn't need to say anything, because somehow I knew he felt my pain.

Chapter Ten

We walked for a while. I welcomed the soft breeze on my face after such extremes of emotion. I felt worn out and it was not long before he suggested we stop for the night. Time had gone so fast I hadn't even noticed the day come to an end. Sam made a fire and we settled down. The stars pierced the dark cover of night, and in the distance I could hear a dog barking. I watched the sparks spitting from the fire, as they rose up into the night sky and eventually disappeared.

"Sam, where are we going, or is that also a secret?"

"No, Alex, we are going on a journey and it's not a secret, but how and when we arrive at our destination is up to you."

"Can you tell me what happened to Noisulli? I remember something about being on a horse and breaking my ribs, the rest is a bit vague."

"Sorry, Alex, can't help you. Maybe it was just a dream."

I knew it couldn't be a dream, if it was then it was very real. The truth is I didn't want it to be a dream. I liked her, she was a beautiful woman. I remember how good it felt to hold her. I could still smell her on my clothes. It had to be real otherwise how could that be explained? I didn't argue the point, but as I fell asleep under the cover of night by the warmth of the fire, I thought of nothing else but Noisulli.

I woke up to the smell of fresh coffee. Sitting up slowly, I rubbed my eyes and stretched my aching limbs. The fact that I didn't remember Sam carrying any supplies with him didn't even make me question where he had got them from. In the grand scheme of things, this was just another one of those, "Of course, why not?" incidents in this whole weird scenario.

WHEN THE STUDENT IS READY THE MASTER WILL APPEAR

"Morning, Alex. Do you want some coffee?"
"Sure, why not? So I am still in this strange dream then?"
"If you want to call it that."
"And you are still my grandfather, but you're not, and this is all so perfect?"
My sarcasm was as effective as spitting into the wind; it appeared to fall on deaf ears. He was staring into the fire while making the coffee, and without looking up he fired a broadside in retaliation to my previous sarcasm.
"The problem is you are all so intent on being perfect, you feel that if you commit what you call a sin, then you are not worthy to talk to God, therefore you don't hear him when he talks to you. This, ironically, is a greater sin, that you deny him and think you are beyond saving. No one or nothing is perfect. Everything is in a state of growth and change."
"Yes, but surely God is perfect?"
"God is only perfect when your perception of him is perfect."
"I don't understand."
"How can I explain this? OK, take a cup with a crack in it. Would you say that it's perfect?"
"No."
"Now let's say that all had cups had cracks. Which one would be more perfect?"
"None, because we would all be the same."
"Alex, you have the gift of free will, and part of free will is discovering your own imperfection. What do you do when you discover this? Do you try to change it? No, you consider yourself unworthy and stop talking to God, because you think he will stop loving you because you aren't perfect.
"I tell you this. The man, woman or child that seeks God, even though they are imperfect, has found perfection."
"But what about the Hindu or the Buddhist? Is their God different from our God? And, if so, have we got it all wrong? Are we worshiping and following the wrong God?"
"There is only one God. If a man's name in English is Alex and in

Russian, Alexandra, does this mean he is a different man? No, he remains the same man. So if one race decides to call him or her by a different name, does this make it a different God?

"No, it doesn't. There are many different flowers in the world but they are all flowers."

"So why do we kill and fight each other? And say my God is the true God when, according to you, this is not so?"

"Because you think that you own God, as you think you own everything in your life, even your children. Do you really think the soul of a child belongs to you? A child is a gift in your care not a possession."

"Hold on, let me get this right. Are you saying that I own nothing, and that if someone wants to come and take something that belongs to me, it's OK?"

"Yes."

"But how can that be? If I work my guts out everyday to achieve what I have, you are saying that anyone can just come and say, 'Thank you very much, I think I will have that'? I don't think that's right."

"Tell me, Alex, do you believe you own your own house?"

"You bet I do. I worked hard to pay the mortgage, and I will be dammed if I will let someone just come and take my house away from me."

"Interesting wording, because you do damn yourself by putting so much attachment into such things. Tell me, the ground your house stands on, do you own this?"

"Now you are just being petty."

"Just answer the question."

"Yes, of course I own the ground."

"I see, and how deep down does your ownership go? In fact, come to think of it, how high into the sky do you own it? Can you see you are just a traveller passing through? The more you carry in your rucksack the slower your journey will be."

"So you are saying I should give up all my possessions and wear a loincloth?"

WHEN THE STUDENT IS READY THE MASTER WILL APPEAR

"A loincloth would be cold and most likely impractical. What I am saying is you should give up attachment. When you do this no one will come and take what you perceive as yours, because they will also know it does not belong to them.

"Do you want some coffee?"

"No, I don't need it but I will have some."

"My word, I think he gets it!"

Chapter Eleven

The landscape was rugged and the trees were small. I was sure I had seen trees like these before but I didn't know where.

Now and again the wind would lift up some of the dry earth into the air; it was like having a hot hairdryer blowing gently on your face. A ride in an air-conditioned car would be great just about now, but I knew that things around here tended to happen the opposite way I wanted them to.

"What kind of trees are these, Sam?"

"Olive trees."

I must have seen them on a television programme, probably a nature channel. They really looked familiar. I hadn't been to any country that grew olive trees, yet even the smell in the air and the rough terrain were familiar.

"Sam, this whole thing is still so strange, and I am not sure if this is a dream or reality, so why do I get the feeling that I recognise this place?"

"Alex, the whole of life is a process of remembering what we already know."

"But I have never been here before. So how can I remember?"

"Don't you mean in this lifetime?"

"No, I mean my life. Oh, I see, the reincarnation debate."

"If that is what you want to call it."

"No, I don't believe in that stuff. You live, you die and then lights out, show over."

"I see."

"Is that it? Aren't you going to argue with me?"

"No."

WHEN THE STUDENT IS READY THE MASTER WILL APPEAR

"Hold on, so far you have argued every point I have made."
"Have I?"
"Yes, you have, and as for lectures, you should have been a college professor."
"Maybe I was."
"So explain reincarnation."
"There isn't really much to explain. According to you it's lights out and that's it."
"Yeah, but you don't have to agree with me. Go on, challenge me."
"Your reality is your perception. Why would I want to change that? So far it has served you well and it's not my place to alter this."
"So you believe in reincarnation."
"It's not what I believe that's important. What is important is whether the current belief you have expresses who you are."
"Yes, because it's a fact."
"Good, then be happy with this fact."
"But you don't believe it."
"You didn't ask me if I believed what you believe. You asked, 'Did I believe in reincarnation?'"
"OK. Do you believe what I believe, that it's a one-shot deal?"
"Yes."
"Hold on. You believe it's a one-shot deal but you believe in reincarnation. That's not possible. Someone believes or doesn't believe in something."
"Really? According to whose opinion?"
"Well, let's just start with everyone in the world."
"Is that so? Then why is it that most of the religions in your world have written that it is wrong to kill, yet you still kill. Is this not the same thing? On one hand you say it's right and then on the other hand it's wrong. Do I not have the right to believe and not believe?"
"Now you are just playing with words."
"Since the dawn of what you term 'civilized man' you have called out, 'For God and country' as you rush into battle, and in his name you have butchered and killed countless millions, and then you say,

'Thou shall not kill.' One day you will all finally understand that you can't kill the soul of a person, be they man, woman or child, but until then I will believe and not believe as you do, and when this no longer serves me I will form new beliefs."

It was like a game of chess and I had the feeling I was being out manoeuvred. It's disconcerting to have your inner self exposed and left out to the elements, and, what's more, to silently come to the realization that a truth you held to be true may be riddled with lies.

Chapter Twelve

You might think it strange, if you were in my situation. You may even question your sanity. Would you really follow a stranger, albeit that he was a facsimile of a dear departed relative? Why didn't I run away, slap my self until I woke up or just turn and walk away?

I suppose a simple analogy is why do you cover your eyes during a horror film but still peek between your fingers? Come to think of it, why go to the horror film in the first place? The reason is, you are curious to see what happens and how it ends. It's why man went to the moon, discovered unknown countries, and longs to travel into space, even though we know our very lives may be in mortal danger.

So on I went, not knowing if I was talking to a ghost or having some strange encounter. Maybe, when I was in the woods in my frantic state, I had forgotten that I had eaten some sort of hallucinogenic mushroom. Alternatively, was I still lying comfortably in my bed at home and this was all a dream.

So right or wrong, I decided I had nothing to lose, and anyway it was more exciting than trying to get a hamburger that actually looked like its picture.

The sun was reaching what my father used to call the yardarm, which was a way of saying it was time to have a drink. It was certainly too hot to be outside, and I was very thirsty. We had also been walking for a few hours, and my feet were starting to ache. In this place nothing would surprise me, so when we came across a small stone building I didn't give it a second thought. The fact that it looked like a cattle shed was a bit unusual, though. I expected to also see a swimming pool. This would have fitted with what I felt a psychedelic sixties trip must be like, certainly a little better than a common old cowshed. As we got closer to the building I could see that behind it was another stone construction, which, although still simple in construction, looked more like a house.

I noticed a man and a woman walking towards us. When they saw Sam, they rushed over and embraced him like a long lost friend who had been away for years. Maybe they were relatives of his? However, when he introduced me, their reaction was strange.

"Simon, Elizabeth, this is my good friend, Alex."

At first, it was as if they had seen a ghost. They just stood still, not saying a word, but when they looked at Sam and he smiled, they embraced me in the same way. I couldn't move my arms, as they were pinned to my side. I didn't know what Simon's occupation was but he had the grip of a bear and, as for Elizabeth, she was not far behind him. Yet her frame was petite and she had the most angelic face. She reminded me of Noisulli, with that same gentle manner, but you knew she also had an inner physical strength to match any man. I remember once doing t'ai chi, a gentle martial art, and coming across this sort of strength, but usually this was attained by many years of practice, and only then could you be called a master. I am not what you would call a touchy, feely sort of person, and all this hugging made me feel a little uncomfortable. It usually takes me years to feel comfortable enough with someone to allow hugging like this. I didn't want to offend them, so what could I do but smile and pretend it was the most natural thing in the world to me.

"You must be thirsty," said Elizabeth. "Come inside, you are welcome in our home. Let me fetch you something to drink."

What I had previously thought was a cattle shed was, in fact, part of their ever so humble home. I had to duck my head to get through the door. Inside it was cool and it felt good to be out of the searing heat of the sun. The room was rustic in appearance, with uneven walls that were whitewashed. Hanging from the exposed timber ceiling were dried-out grapevines. Every now and then, in small recesses in the walls, were placed small white candles. The floor was laid out with thick flagstone tiles, which felt cool beneath my feet,

WHEN THE STUDENT IS READY THE MASTER WILL APPEAR

even though I was wearing shoes. It wasn't long before Elizabeth returned with a stone jug and some clay cups. She filled the cups with cold water, and I was looking forward to finally quenching my thirst. As I tipped my head back to drink, it felt like someone was taking my shoes off. I looked down thinking it was just my imagination playing a trick on me, but it wasn't. Elizabeth had taken my shoes off, and was preparing to wash my feet.

"No, it's OK, really," I said. "I can do that."

"Relax, Alex," said Sam. "It's the custom in these parts."

Elizabeth pulled a bowl of water towards her and started washing my feet. I hadn't realized how hot they were. They were covered in dirt, which had got into my shoes, from walking around this dusty landscape. The cold water felt good but I was embarrassed that a stranger would do such a thing for me.

She dried my feet and then started doing the same thing to Sam, but to my surprise he stood up and instead washed her feet. What was going on? Was this some kind of foot fetish party? Whoa, talk about flashback. All of a sudden I became very light-headed. Simon managed to catch me just as my legs gave way beneath me and I fell.

"Alex, are you OK?" said Simon.

"I think so; it must be too much sun. I was looking at Sam's feet and the next moment they were covered in blood. Then I had this sudden head rush and next thing I know you caught me. I'm really sorry, but if you knew the day I have had you would understand."

"When did you last eat?" asked Elizabeth.

"You know, I couldn't tell you. I haven't really felt hungry. Maybe you are right, I should really eat something."

The fact is I was going through the motions of drinking because I had been offered it, but was I actually thirsty? And was I really hungry? Now though, as I thought about it, I suddenly had an appetite, and my mouth felt very dry.

"Well, you put your feet up and relax. It's not good to be walking at this time of the day in this heat," said Elizabeth.

Elizabeth got me what looked like a milking stool and lifted my legs up onto it.

"Now you just sit there and I will get you something to eat."

"Thank you. That's very kind of you."

I felt like I had known these people for years; it was like I had just been down the road to buy some bread, and it felt like the most natural thing in the world to be sitting here talking to them. Simon also got up.

"Come on, Elizabeth, I will help you."

They both disappeared into another room to prepare some food for us.

I leaned over to Sam and whispered, "What the hell is going on? What was all that foot cleaning stuff? And I swear your feet were covered in blood, but don't ask me to testify to it in court because I will deny it."

"I told you. They were just washing my feet."

"Look, you may look like my grandfather, and God knows how, but there was more than just foot washing going on here."

"Yes, you are right. God does know how but, really, it's just the custom around here to wash the feet of weary travellers you invite into your home."

"Right, and I am the Pope."

"Really? I thought I had seen you before somewhere."

"Yeah, very funny."

Chapter Thirteen

Simon and Elizabeth returned with some food, and I pulled away quickly from Sam as I didn't want them to think I was whispering about them. I also didn't want to offend them. Who knows, if washing strangers' feet is normal, what's to say that whispering may be considered highly offensive.

To eat when you are really hungry is a pleasure. Often, though, I just ate because it was breakfast time or midday.

I would say to myself, "It's lunchtime and I had better eat something." And as for supper, no wonder I had problems sleeping. I always ate so much at night, and half the time I wasn't even hungry.

This time it was different. I was hungry and my body was crying out for food. Everything they gave me to eat was so full of taste; it was like eating food for the first time in my life. This surprised me, as the meal was very simple and nothing out of the ordinary. I don't think I had ever tasted such food like this before. The bread was flat and made from coarse, home-ground flour, and the smell of it filled the room. Even the water tasted amazing. The sweet, juicy tomatoes burst in my mouth, sending my taste buds wild.

I guess this is what happens when you grow your own food.

"Would you like some wine?" asked Simon.

"Thank you. That would be nice." I couldn't wait to taste it, if everything else tasted so good what would the wine taste like?

He passed the jug of wine to Sam and he poured us each a cup.

"Alex," said Sam, "have some bread. If you dip it in the wine you will find it quenches your thirst."

We all dipped the amazing bread into the wine, and he was right, it did quench the thirst.

"Simon, it has a strange sort of taste. What kind of grapes do you use?"

"Nothing special, but you are right, it does taste a little different today. I find when I am thirsty it always tastes better, and today is an exceptionally hot day."

It was good, and I made a mental note to myself to drink wine like this again. That's if I ever got home. But where was home?

The house reminded me of France; was France my home? It was constructed from the same rough stone, which was in plentiful supply. All you had to do was walk outside and pick it up. It was amazing that anything grew in this hot and rugged landscape. I felt a bit awkward asking my hosts what they did for a living, but nonetheless my curiosity always got the better of me. My mother said it started in childhood, when I was always taking things apart to see how they worked. The problem was, I could never put them back together, and somehow always ended up with extra screws.

"We harvest the olives and we also have some vines."

"Sounds like hard work. How do you cope with this heat?"

"Actually, we are used to it and we always have plenty of help."

"So you have a family then."

"No, we have help from a good friend. He usually sends us a couple of workers."

Elizabeth, who had not really said that much until this point, perked up.

"Yes, real angels they are. Such a Godsend." Then they all started laughing.

"What? Did I miss something?"

"No, it's OK, Alex," said Sam. "It's just that Elizabeth has a wonderful way with words, and she is right, they really are a Godsend."

"Oh, OK." I still didn't get it.

However, I knew from my own experience that sometimes when old friends got together and talked about the past, newcomers were not privy to the in-jokes. So I just pretended that I understood what they were laughing about, and didn't try to understand.

WHEN THE STUDENT IS READY THE MASTER WILL APPEAR

The laughing died down and Elizabeth said, "So, Alex, where are you and Sam going?"

"Good question. Maybe you should ask my guide. By the way, did I tell you he looks just like my grandfather?"

"Really? That's interesting. Was he also a teacher?"

"No, why do you say that?"

"Oh, I thought that Sam would have told you he was a teacher."

"No, he didn't actually." I turned to face him. I felt like a child who had just discovered a big secret.

"So Sam," I said with a smile on my face, "you're a teacher."

"Elizabeth is just being kind and it's very flattering of her, but I like to think of myself more as a person who guides people. Teacher is such an official term; are we not all teachers in our own way? Now if you want a good teacher, Alex is your man."

"Me? You must be joking. I am not a teacher!"

"Oh, I thought you were, Alex. Sorry, my mistake. So what is it you actually do then?" Now it was Sam's turn to tease me.

"That's a good question."

I thought about it, but it was like having amnesia and trying to see through a thick fog. I knew the answer but couldn't quite grasp it.

I felt a little embarrassed at not being able to remember what it was I did.

"You know, it's funny. I don't know what I do. I know I keep blaming the heat, but it's like every time I try to remember I forget even more. In fact, I can't really remember much about anything. The only thing that stays with me is this vision of a girl and a horse."

"Yes," said Simon. "I remember visions of girls."

Elizabeth gave him a nudge in the ribs, "Just you remember I am the only vision you should be seeing, and lucky you are to have me."

You could tell they had one of those relationships that many envy. I am sure they had their ups and downs, but you knew they were meant to be together. God willing, they would grow old gracefully and be happy together.

I was still a bit perplexed to discover that I didn't know what it was I did. I felt foolish. How could I not know? Sam could see my forehead screwing up, and knew I was fighting to find the answer.

"Alex, maybe who you are is more important than what you do."

"Are they not the same thing? I am Alex. At least I know this."

"Are you?"

"Yes, I might have forgotten many things but of this I am certain."

"Tell me, when you were a child did Santa Claus exist for you?"

"Yes, of course."

"And when you grew up and you found out he was just a man in a red outfit, did he still exist for you?"

"No."

"And yet you are certain you are Alex. How do you know that one day you might wake up and find out that you don't really exist as you think you do, and, in fact, you are someone else?"

"Because though I might not know where I am at this moment, or whether I just might be having a very realistic dream, one thing is for sure, I know who I am."

"OK, you know who you are, but are you able to consider and accept the possibility you're someone else?"

"Everything is possible, but at this moment in time, no."

"I can settle for that for now, but I want you to remember this conversation, because even the caterpillar has to accept that sooner or later he is really a butterfly."

"All right, and if I find out, and I suspect I will, that I am actually who I say I am, will you promise then to tell me who you are?"

"I will. It's a deal."

Chapter Fourteen

We talked some more about the wine, and Simon shared some of his winemaking secrets with me, on the proviso that I promised to send him a bottle of my first homemade wine.

This was going to be interesting, sending a bottle of wine to a dream or hallucinogenic experience. I was still unable to say whether this place was real or not, but so far things like the food and the environment tasted and appeared to be very real.

I liked Simon, he was a down to earth sort of man. He had hands like shovels and they were ingrained with deep lines from years of working on the land. He had no airs and graces and, if I had time to get to know him better, he would be the sort of person I would have liked as a lifelong friend. I found friendships so transient in the modern world, people hardly stayed in one place long enough to form strong bonds. Most of my friends had been moved about by the multinational companies they worked for. Sometimes even to different countries, so I found that I only knew about five people that I could really call friends, whereas the others were more acquaintances. I remember my sister once saying to me…Hold on, I have a sister?

"Sam, I just remembered I have a sister."

"You see, you just stop trying and you remember."

"I also have friends who work for big companies."

I lost my train of thought but it didn't matter. To remember something made me feel good, but at the same time a bit insecure. What if Sam was right? What if I suddenly remembered I was not Alex? What if I was someone I didn't really like? This was crazy. If I kept this up I was going to go round the bend.

By now, the heat was becoming a little more bearable, and I felt full and needed to clear my head.

"Thanks for the food, Elizabeth. I need to stretch my legs. Do you mind if I go for a walk?"

"No, not at all. Do you mind if I join you, Alex? I could also do with a walk; it will give Sam and Simon a chance to catch up."

Sometimes I felt like being alone, but I didn't want to offend Elizabeth, especially after she had welcomed me into her home.

"Sure, no problem."

"Good. I will show you the lake, the air is cooler there."

"You have a lake?" I was surprised.

It was as if Simon and Sam had not heard anything Elizabeth and I had said. They were so deep in conversation you would think they were planning a major company takeover.

"See you in a bit," I said.

But they didn't even look up, they just huddled closer together and carried on talking almost in a whisper.

Walking with Elizabeth felt awkward, just like it is with any new person you have just met and have no history with.

We made small talk, and she pointed out various things to me on the way. She told me that soon it would be time to harvest the olives, and that's why there were nets under all the trees, ready to catch them as they fell. The rest were hand-picked, but they had only a short time to harvest them, and she said that you had to have strong hands.

After a short while and further polite conversation, we reached the brow of a hill, and what I saw before me took my breath away.

Stretching out as far as the eye could see was a lake, but not just any old lake. There were people on it fishing and hauling in great big nets, full to the brim with fish. As the sun hit the nets they sparkled as if they were incrusted with diamonds, as each drop of water acted like a tiny prism. The clothes that the people were wearing were also very different, and many of them were barefoot. It was as if, in the midst of this desolate land, life had sprung forth with a mighty explosion and poured its bounty upon the earth. I was happy to see so many people, and I didn't even try to understand their appearance, I was just glad not to feel alone.

WHEN THE STUDENT IS READY THE MASTER WILL APPEAR

Elizabeth and I made our way down the hill towards the lakeside. As we got closer I could hear the sound of many voices intermingling into one, almost unified, hum, like a colony of bees. Then one voice called out through the crowd.

"Elizabeth."

Standing on a boat and holding onto the mast, as he waved with his other hand, was a bearded man.

"Elizabeth, over here," he shouted again, this time a little louder.

We jostled our way through the people, avoiding the piles of fish being sold and bartered on the lakeside. When we finally reached him the two of them hugged each other, then Elizabeth turned to me.

"Peter, this is Alex. He is travelling with Sam."

"Sam?" Peter asked. He appeared a bit perplexed as if he didn't know who she was talking about; it was exactly the same way Simon and Elizabeth had reacted when I first mentioned his name.

She gave him a frustrated look like someone trying to say something, but who can only communicate using hand gestures.

"Oh, Sam. Sorry, it's all this noise. We had such a good catch today; it's caused a great deal of excitement.

"Nice to meet you, Alex. Any friend of Sam's is a friend of mine."

Peter shook my hand. What was it about these people? They all had grips like iron, even the women. I attempted to do the manly thing and give a firm grip in response, but I'm sure Peter hardly noticed.

"So don't you usually catch this many fish?"

"We always get a good catch, but today is exceptionally good. Which is always cause for celebration, it means tonight there will be a feast. You must come."

"That's very kind of you but I am a stranger to this place."

"No such thing. Elizabeth, tell him he must come."

"Yes, Alex, you must. Sam and Simon will also be there."

"Ok, why not, and I'm sure I can get Simon to reveal a few more of his winemaking secrets."

"Good, then it's settled. So, Alex, are you a sailor?"

"There was a time when I could have answered that question but, to be honest, I don't know."

"In that case there is one way to find out. Elizabeth, do you mind if I steal your friend away from you for a bit?"

"No, go ahead. I need to get some fish and I want to see if Mary is going tonight. I'll meet you here, but if I'm not back when you return, will you take Alex back to my house?"

"Sure. No problem."

Again it was as if my life did not belong to me. It looked like I was going with Peter whether I liked it or not.

Chapter Fifteen

"Climb aboard, Alex," said Peter.
Peter held my hand, and his grip was as sure and strong as before. Steadying myself with my other hand I climbed aboard. The boat's construction was very simple, and it only had one sail. The outside was painted white with a blue line running down the length of the hull. Peter was barefoot, and he walked around the boat as if he was as comfortable on water as on land.
"Here, Alex, you sit at the bow. You will get a better view from there."
"Peter," a man called from the shore, "are you going out to get some more fish?"
"No, John, but I might be catching something else. Push us out, will you?"
The man waded into the water and gave the boat a push. Peter hoisted the sail up and it fluttered into life like a new fledgling discovering its wings for the first time.
The boat gracefully glided out from the lakeside. I closed my eyes and soaked in the gentle afternoon sun.
The cool wind blowing in off the lake and the motion of the boat was hypnotic. I leaned forward to trail my hand in the water. The sunlight danced across the surface in shimmering patterns, like a veil of silk.
"Watch out for the crocodiles," said Peter.
I snapped my hand out of the water and pulled myself upright. Peter laughed.
"Don't worry, there aren't any crocodiles. I was only joking, the piranhas ate them all."

I leaned forward again putting my hand back in the water.

I was at peace and I didn't care who I was, or where I was going. I was what you might call living in the perfect moment, something I had tried to do for so long, but never found the time, and there was the irony.

After a while we appeared to slow down, so I turned to see why, and as I did I was no longer in that perfect moment, but once again instantly scared and confused.

I was completely alone, and Peter was nowhere to be seen. Frantically I looked around to see if he had fallen into the water, but I couldn't see him, not a splash or even a bubble. The water was as calm as if it had been frozen.

I stood up, at the same time trying hard to keep my balance, hoping I could call to the shore for help, but there was no one there.

What had happened to all the people? One minute I was in paradise and the next hell. Who was screwing with my mind? Please God, get me out of this nightmare.

At first I thought it was a seagull, as a white speck appeared on the horizon, but as it got closer I noticed it was a man dressed in a white robe. I closed my eyes in the hope that when I opened them again things would return to normal.

"No, this is not real," I kept saying to myself but, when I looked again, he was getting closer and closer. It was Sam. What the hell was he doing? He was walking on the water. I wanted to jump overboard and swim to shore. Even though I was confused and scared, I was still able to figure I would need to be an Olympic swimmer to get there.

So then I said the most stupid and ridiculous thing.

"Hi, Sam. Good to see you. Oh, and by the way, did you know you were walking on water?" When in doubt use sarcasm, but could you blame me, what else could I do?

"Yes, Alex, I suppose I am."

"You suppose you are. Oh, I will just have a pound of potatoes, some tomatoes and, while you're at it, do you happen to sell a book about this big, by this wide, that's called *The Answer to Mind Fuck-ups*? "What do you mean 'I suppose I am?' People don't just walk on water, and what happened to Peter? Did you whack him? Is he swimming with the fishes?"

"OK, Alex, enough of the godfather impressions. It's all very normal. I can explain everything."

"Really? That's good. So how about you explain it all to me now?"

"I think that's fair. You deserve at least that."

"Finally I am going to get some answers!"

"You see, Alex, everyone can walk on water."

"Aaaaa, I knew it. I knew you weren't going to give me a straight explanation. That would be too predictable and simple."

"If you will just calm down for a second it will all become clear. Well, most of it."

"Oh, and which bit won't be so clear?"

"That's the bit that's up to you. I can tell you anything you want, except who you are, that's the bit you have to figure out for yourself."

"So is that what you and Simon were whispering about?"

"Yes, sorry about that, but we had to decide how best to help you."

"I knew it. You know my father always said trust your instincts, they are usually ninety-nine percent right. Great! Now I remember what my father said."

"Yes, and he was right."

"OK, let me get this straight. I can ask anything but who I am, except I know who I am, so I don't really need to ask that anyway. My first question is, 'Where am I?'"

"You are in what you might call heaven."

"Am I dead?"

"Yes and no."

"Am I dead or am I alive? It's a simple question." My mind was swimming around, my body felt like it was full of electricity, able only to contain a certain critical amount before it exploded.

"OK, you are alive, but you can't die."

"I'm immortal, is that what you are saying?"

"Yes, I suppose you could call it that."

"So what about Peter and the boat, Simon and Elizabeth? Are you saying it's all heaven?"

"Yes."

"So is that why the food and wine tasted so good? I knew there was something different about how it tasted. So if this is heaven why do we need to eat?"

"You don't, but we find that it reminds us of our time in the physical form. It's more about coming together to share."

"And you, who are you, are you really my grandfather?"

"Ah well, that's one you will have to figure out for yourself."

"I thought you said I could ask anything and get an answer, except who you thought I was, which is bullshit and you know it, because I am Alex alive or dead."

"Yes, but in finding out who I am you will know who you are, and so I can't give you that answer."

"So you are not my grandfather then?"

"No, I am afraid not, but he is here."

"So why do you look like him? Why the disguise?"

"Because we find it easier to appear at first as loved ones, it's less of a shock this way for the returning soul."

"Hold on, you said 'we.' Does that mean there are many people doing this frightening the living shit out of people thing? Why don't you just do it en masse and get it over with? Is there some kind of gratification you get from messing with people's minds?"

"Alex, do you truly believe you have a mind?"

"Yes, as strange as it may be to you, yes I do."

"Well, my friend, hold onto your reality because you no longer have a mind. As you move from one vibration to another, there are certain parts of you in what you call reality that no longer serve a purpose to your illusion."

"So if I don't," I paused. "Excuse me, would you mind getting into the boat? It's a bit off-putting you just standing there on the water."

"Sure, if it makes you feel better."

"Yes, it does."

Sam, or whoever he was, climbed into the boat and it made me feel a little easier. If I was going crazy I wanted to go crazy sanely.

"So is this my body?"

"No, your body is still in the reality you call earth, and though you may not remember, your body has been injured. You are in a privileged position, Alex. Not many have your choice to stay or return to physical form."

"But why me? What is so special about me?"

"All souls are special, but once in a while there is a soul who shines that little bit brighter."

"Don't tell me that's me?"

"Yes. Is that so awful?"

"No, except I haven't done anything heroic in my life. No leaping from tall buildings nor rescuing children from burning buildings, no Nobel Peace Prize for discovering the cure to some life-threatening disease, so please take this label off me. I don't even believe in a life after death."

"There was once a time when you did. There was once a time that you did something so heroic it changed the course of history. It caused the start of an event that touched the hearts of millions of men, women and children. And for centuries they didn't even know it. In fact, you do not even know it, but now is the time, Alex, for you to discover who you really are."

"I think you have me mixed up with Mother Teresa or Gandhi. I think if I had done what you think I have done I would remember."

"Not so. In fact, you chose to forget and that made me sad, so I have decided it is time to set the record straight."

"So does that mean you are going to let the whole world know?"

"No, just you, because you were created with free will and that means you must find out for yourself. However, that doesn't mean I can't steer you in the right direction, for even God the Almighty in his wisdom wouldn't let one of his flock suffer the self-persecution that the world has placed upon your shoulders, so he has sent me to set you free."

"Well, that's very nice of him I must say, because so far my life has been no bed of roses. Maybe that explains my car being repossessed, struggling to pay the mortgage, and a failed marriage, and what you are saying is it's all my fault."

"No, Alex. You have been hurting yourself because you knew no other way. You did something that you thought was so evil that for centuries you have been persecuting yourself. When God has tried to call you home you wouldn't listen, so now he has sent me to lead you back to him."

"And how do you propose to do this?"

"There is a place I would like to take you to. It will take us some time to get there, but I think, when you see it, then you will remember who you are."

"I don't get it. If this is really heaven why can't we just do the beam-me-up Scotty thing, and then I can see this place now?"

"I have always loved your humour, Alex. You still haven't lost it and, as lame as it sounds, there is truth in the saying, 'It's not what you find, but the journey that you take.' I think on this journey it is better that you discover slowly. As I have said to you before, your greatest secret is who you really are."

"I thought the journey had already started. Where have we been going all this time?"

"To this point you are right now. This is your moment of realization, the point where you can choose to go left or right."

"But what if I go left and it's the wrong turn?"

"There are no right or wrong turns, Alex, just different paths all leading to the same point. If a man takes a bike to a city and another man takes a car, they will both get there, except one will get there quicker than the other."

"So let me just run this by you again. I am dead but I am not, I am not who I think I am, and I have done something that affected the whole world, but I don't remember what it is."

"Yes, that's about right, but don't forget the part where you have been needlessly persecuting yourself for centuries."

"Oh yes, how could I forget that?"

"So how about we walk back to shore, or would you feel more comfortable going by boat?"

WHEN THE STUDENT IS READY THE MASTER WILL APPEAR

"If you don't mind I think I will leave the walking on water to you, and I will take the boat."

He came and sat beside me and put his hand on my shoulder, "Don't worry, you are in no danger. Close your eyes for a minute."

So I closed my eyes, and when he asked me to open them again Peter reappeared, and when I looked to shore, all the people were there, just as before, going about their business as if nothing had happened.

"What was all that about?" I asked.

"What was what all about?" he asked, as if everything was normal.

"That disappearing and reappearing thing."

"Oh, that. I thought we should be alone when I told you where you were. I didn't want you to be distracted."

Chapter Sixteen

We sailed into shore and Elizabeth greeted us. Peter threw her the rope and she tied the boat up.

"I've got us a nice bit of fish for supper," she said. "So did you tell him?"

"Yes. I don't think he believes me though, but when he tastes how good your fish supper is, he will know he is in heaven."

They both laughed, which made me feel a little uneasy, but what could I do? I had nowhere to go, and I didn't know if I was dead or alive, or even what had happened to me.

My memory was all over the place. I kept remembering and forgetting things. I knew that I had a failed marriage and a mortgage. I started wondering if I had any children. I couldn't feel anything; it was as if my whole body was numb. I didn't even know if I had a body. Suddenly I had so many questions and no answers.

I could have asked any question that night at the feast, as we sat there around the table eating Elizabeth's fantastic fish supper.

I could have asked for the answer to the cure for cancer, but no, instead I asked Sam, "So what's with the robe? You look like an Arab dressed like that."

"It's more comfortable and it's how you perceive me."

"I didn't ask you to dress like that."

"As you start to remember who you are, things will start to change, especially your immediate surroundings and the people close to you. What was familiar to you in the past will become stronger in the present."

"Is that why I have been forgetting then remembering things?"

"Yes, because you are still not detached from your physical body.

WHEN THE STUDENT IS READY THE MASTER WILL APPEAR

You keep shifting between two realities. Usually when a person's body fails to function they make a complete break, but you haven't yet decided if you want to let go."

"What if a person meets a sudden and violent end?"

"In this case they would be taken from their body very quickly, but only at the last second. Although time does not exist, I talk of things in your reality. The soul knows it is going to leave the body."

"Are you saying we all know when we are going to die?"

"Yes, but you have chosen not to remember. Death is an experience as life is an experience; it's just another phase of your existence."

"I can't believe this. That means that life is preordained.

"So why do people bother getting old at all, and suffer in pain with disease like arthritis, and yet others die so young? What about those poor children that are born disabled?"

"Why do you look at these conditions and say they are so bad?"

"Because I have seen people who are disabled, and I have seen people in such pain with arthritis they can hardly move. Don't tell me these are good conditions."

"If a soul makes the decision to come into physical matter it's not done lightly, but it is done willingly and with joy. The soul knows that life is an internal cycle of being born and dying. When the physical body dies the soul is released and born into spirit. When a soul comes into the physical it is also born, so you see there is no death. The answer to your question, therefore, is perceived from a distorted reality. Please forgive me, I don't mean to belittle you, but has it ever occurred to you that those that suffer the most in the physical form, have chosen to do so and, in fact, through their perceived suffering grow faster than those who appear to live a charmed life. Have you not been told many times in your life that God only gives you that which he thinks you can carry? Did you not also realize that maybe this was the exact point in time you needed to hear this? I have also said to you many times before you have free will and, therefore, you also carry that which you have chosen to experience."

"Then it's true that suffering brings you closer to God?
"So should we whip our selves with branches and wear sackcloth? I can't see any love in that."
"The moment a soul decides it no longer wants an experience then the experience stops."
"So a child in a wheelchair unable to move or talk; are you saying that if that child chose to no longer experience that restrictive state it would stop?"
"Why do you insist on seeing yourself as better than a disabled child?"
"I don't."
"I think you do. You are assuming that the child is worse off than you, which in turn implies you are better off and, therefore, better than that child. Don't you see what great courage it takes for a soul to make the conscious decision to come into a restrictive physical form, and don't you also see what great teachers these souls who you perceive to suffer are?"
"Now I feel guilty."
"No, now you understand. You see like a child who struggles day in, day out to grasp the meaning of a subject, then one day without any apparent reason, hey presto, he or she gets it. You are that child. All that has happened is now you get it, and of course the other difference for you now is you are in a class where all the children get it as well.
"Do you remember when you were younger in your physical life, and you looked after a disabled man while he was in hospital? How, since a child, his parents had looked after him every single day of his life?"
"Yes, I remember him. He was admitted into hospital with cancer; it was the first time they had been parted from him in forty years. I remember how tired they looked, and how dedicated they were to him."
"And do you also remember what happened when he passed away?"
"Yes, they were very angry with the hospital and started saying he

had received poor nursing care. Which was not true, because I worked with those people and they did their best, doing everything humanly possible to make sure he passed peacefully when it was time for him to go."

"Well, did you know he was a great teacher? He taught them what it was to love someone your whole life unconditionally, even if to the outside world he appeared imperfect. They were angry when he parted, not because he had received poor nursing care as they had thought, but because they had graduated and the lesson was over. Their teacher had to go and he had decided it was time for them to go out into the world."

"I have often wondered what happened to them after he died. Do you know?"

"Yes, they spent the remainder of their lives helping others in the same situation, with disabled or ill children, to see how special the children are. And, when it was finally their time to leave the world, the three of them were together again and they saw how perfect the lesson had been."

"I still feel guilty. How could I have been so superior? My pity was false and wasted. How many teachers have I passed by? What other opportunities have I missed just because I failed to see past my perception of perfection?"

"You would be right, but for one thing, though."

"And what is that?"

"You assume that you have never lived a life as a disabled or ill person, and you also forget that you have also been a teacher. In fact, when you discover who you really are you will see what a great teacher you have been."

Chapter Seventeen

The fish arrived but this time instead of feeling hungry, as I had before, I felt nothing. There was no saliva in my mouth at the anticipation of eating what looked like a delicious meal, and it was not because I felt sick; it was just that I felt nothing, as if I would never have to eat again, and I would still be all right. Elizabeth could see my hesitation and looked at Sam as if to say, "Explain to him."

"Oh, sorry," he said. "I should have told you. After you have been here for a while, Alex, and you adjust to this new experience, you will start to feel different. Your body, although at first may appear the same, but, in fact, is very different. One of the things you will find is that you no longer have an appetite, because you no longer need food to sustain your life force."

I thought this was strange as they were all sitting around the table just about to eat a fish supper. Why were they going to eat if they did not need to?

"So why are you eating then? What's the point?"

"We eat, not because we need to have food, but because we choose to. For us it's more of a celebration in remembrance of the times we spent together in a previous life, and so we choose to feel hunger. Every meal here is not just about eating, it's about coming together and sharing. There was a time in your earth history when people did this but, as your pace of life got faster and people had less time, eating just became another thing to do. So here we like to remember and affirm our friendship by sharing a meal together. This is not the same for all, some share in different ways, but eating here is more a sociable thing."

"OK, I can understand that, but no one can eat if they are not

WHEN THE STUDENT IS READY THE MASTER WILL APPEAR

hungry. I know it's possible but it's not enjoyable."

"But we are hungry. In fact, you can be hungry too, all you have to do is decide you are hungry and you will be."

"How do you decide you are hungry? Isn't hunger a feeling?"

"Yes, but before that feeling comes a thought. Close your eyes and think of being hungry, think about what it feels like."

So I closed my eyes and what I thought was going to be simple was, in fact, very hard. I was so used to hunger being an automatic reaction. In the past my mouth would salivate, my stomach would feel empty, and I knew I needed food, but breaking down these feelings was not that simple.

"This is hard," I said. "I still don't feel hungry."

"It takes a little practice. In this place all actions are conscious. Try not to think of your feelings, but rather the relationship you have with food."

"What do you mean the relationship I have with food? This is not a blind date you know."

They all smiled and were obviously amused by my reaction to the idea that I should have a relationship with food.

"Before you came here it was about being reactive. You felt hungry and you ate, but here you need to think about the food, about it being a part of you.

"Imagine it as becoming part of you as a life-giving force, learn to respect it. On earth you put things into your body without thinking what they would do to you."

He handed me a piece of fish and though I was still not feeling hungry I took it.

"Now put it into your mouth but don't just be reactive and chew it, let it just sit in your mouth for a bit."

So I put the fish in my mouth and, instead of chewing it as I would have done in the past, I did as Sam said and held it there.

Mumbling through a mouth full of fish I managed to just about talk.

"Now what?"

"Now close your eyes and imagine the molecules that make up the fish, feel the texture, see them as living and moving. Imagine, like a jigsaw puzzle, how the parts of the fish and the parts of your body come together to give you energy and life. Now feel that life flowing through your body."

My mouth was instantly awash with taste. I could taste each part of the fish, the herbs it was dressed with, the softness of the butter. It crumbled and dissolved inside me. It was an explosion of exquisite taste.

"Wow, that was amazing, but a lot of hard work just to eat!"

"You will get used to it. After a while you will never look at food again in the same way, and you will only eat when you choose to."

"But where does the food go once it's inside you?"

"It does not need to go anywhere because it is not separate from you. When you pick up food and you see it outside of yourself, that's just an illusion. In this place you call heaven nothing is separate, so nothing is ever outside of you. When you eat it's just like breathing. However, you will experience a sensation when you eat as if your body is tingling, and you will feel light. This is because you are reaffirming your connection with the whole, and the whole is God."

"I'm confused. Why have a body at all? What is the point?"

"Oh, Alex. I wish the others were as quick at learning as you. Do you know it usually takes months for a soul to get to this point of understanding, and ask what you have just asked? Please understand, I use the word 'months' only to give you a point of reference, for, in fact, time does not exist, but that's another lesson. Let me tell you in a way that you can understand, and hopefully you will discover the answer to your question on your own."

He sat in silence for a while looking at the ground. I could hear the night crickets and in the distance a lone owl hooting for its mate. I'm sure if I had gone outside at that moment the stars would have been radiant in the night sky. Bit by bit my perception of reality, as I knew it, was being eroded, and I felt vulnerable.

Still looking down, Sam lifted one hand and pointed to the fireplace. Then, with a matter of fact sweeping gesture of his hand, the fire instantly leapt into life in the hearth. I looked at Simon and

WHEN THE STUDENT IS READY THE MASTER WILL APPEAR

Elizabeth for some explanation, but they appeared to be unaffected by any of this, and just sat there looking at Sam. Eventually he spoke.

"Alex, look into the fire and tell me what you see."

I looked at the fire expecting a face to appear, or for the fire to change colour, but all I saw was the fire and the flames.

"Just flames and sparks. Nothing out of the ordinary."

"And on earth did you think having a body was normal and nothing out of the ordinary, as you say?"

"Yes. It was something I never even thought about; we all have bodies. Those that didn't were six-feet under and could not say much on the subject."

"So you are saying, like the fire, it was normal?"

"Yes."

"Now, Alex, look at the fire again. Tell me if I asked you to pass your hand through the flames what would happen?"

"You mean apart from my flesh melting, and the shrink saying why did you do it?"

"Yes, apart from that."

"Not much. I might feel a little heat but otherwise nothing."

"Yet the flames are really there. You can't touch them or hold them, but they are there. In fact, they could even burn you. Now, what about the sparks?"

"Like the fire they might burn me, but that depends how long they had been apart from the fire. If they had cooled down I might even be able to pick them up."

"So what has this all got to do with anything? Are we having a camping lesson, or will I suddenly have a great revelation about the meaning of life?"

"Alex, do you not remember that it is better to be prepared? For the thief gives no warning when he comes in the quiet of the night."

"OK, sorry, didn't mean to dig you in the ribs, but can't you just tell me why we need to have a body?"

"Did you ever remember any of the algebra you studied at school?"

"No, couldn't stand it. I could never see the point of learning it. I knew what I wanted to be, and it wasn't a mathematician."

"And do you remember childhood stories of goblins and fairies?"

"Yes, tell me a child that does not."

"But you didn't want to be a goblin, and I am sure you would have made a lousy fairy."

"OK. So your point is?"

"My point is, Alex, that we remember things and take them into our soul only when they inspire our imagination. Once in a while a child will be inspired by algebra, and for them it becomes as alive as goblins and fairies. I want you to take what we are talking about into your soul, because you will forget all this if I just give you the answers."

"You said I could ask anything, though."

"And you can, and as promised I will give you the answers, but how I give them to you is up to me."

"Are you sure you have never sold second-hand cars in your previous life, Sam? You would have been very good at it."

"Yes, I'm sure I would have, but for now I am selling information. The question is, are you buying?"

"OK, I give in. Tell me about the fire."

"On earth you say God is all around you, yet you cannot touch him, smell him or even see him, yet you say he is there. You also say that he is the light and the way, and you are not worthy to look upon his face. In fact, even his name is hallowed. The fire, Alex, is like God, you cannot hold it in your hands. Its light is radiant and you love it because it gives you warmth, but you also you fear it, and if you get too close it will burn you. It has the power to sustain life and destroy it."

"I have never thought of God as being destructive, and I never bought into that bit about being born into sin.

"I believe the inner soul of man is essentially good, and that man blames God for his own destructiveness, instead of taking responsibility."

"In part, I agree with you, for when you truly discover who you are, you will see how much you have believed that you are sinful and destructive, and then you will take responsibility. Have you noticed, Alex, that for a man who said he believed you live and die and that's the end of it, you are talking about God a lot?"

"Yeah, yeah, very funny. Shall we get on with the story now?"

"Depending on how long the sparks have been out of the fire, like you said, you may or may not be able to pick them up. The sparks are the body of man, and the further away from God they get the colder they become. However far they decide to go, though, they will always be a part of the fire, because it is the fire that created them. And in each spark are the building blocks of the original fire. Have you noticed that if you take a small spark that becomes a cold ember and place it back in the fire, how quickly it comes to life again? And in seconds you are not even able to see it because it becomes part of the fire again. So, in answer to your question, Alex, why do we need bodies? It is because we have moved away from God and in doing so our vibrations become slower. When we have learnt all we need to learn we return to the fire, and in an instant God's love engulfs us and we burn so bright we cannot be seen. Yet on earth our loved ones say, 'I know he or she is still with me.'"

Chapter Eighteen

I was still, and I remained silent for a while. Again the question of my identity loomed in my mind. But did it?

If I had no mind then where did this feeling come from? And then a realization. I was filled with sadness because of something he had said.

"Sam, apart from never looking at a fire in the same way again, and you are right, I will always remember what you just said and never remember one algebraic question, can you tell me, did the spark leave the fire or was it pushed out?"

"I see, Alex. You are starting to understand the deeper meaning and your instincts are right. This is why you feel sad. No soul who passes over can discover this truth and not be affected by it."

If I understood what he was saying to be correct, then it had to be the biggest blunder man had made since the dawn of time.

"Are you saying we decided to consciously separate from God, to fall away from him? That's crazy, why would a soul do such a thing?"

"Even I cannot answer that one, but I can tell you that all are free to return."

"We were in a five-star hotel, all expenses paid, no bills worries and we decided to live in a mud hut in the middle of nowhere, eking out a living and just about getting by.

"That has to be the most stupid thing we ever did. Were frontal lobotomies a fashion statement in those days?"

"Alex, promise me one thing. If you do decide to return to earth, you need to get a talent agent and become a comic. Don't waste your gift of humour."

We all laughed, something that I was doing a lot of recently. Which was even funnier considering I was half dead, in a room full of people, and also in heaven.

Chapter Nineteen

According to Sam, time did not exist. I didn't really understand this concept, however, I had to admit, time or no time, something was passing very quickly. One moment I was going to sleep, and the next I was getting up. It was as if I had blinked, and somehow eight hours had passed in a second.

"Hold on, Alex, you will be OK. We are almost there."

I opened my eyes and suddenly a sharp pain hit me with such intensity I wanted to vomit. Not again! I was on the horse and I could smell its sweat. She must have been riding it hard to get me to wherever we were going.

"Noisulli, it's good to hear your voice again. I missed you."

"I didn't go anywhere, Alex, you passed out. You keep drifting in and out of consciousness. Try not to talk, we are almost there."

"But I have so much to tell you. Did you know I am not really here?"

"Yes, Alex, whatever you say. Just stop talking and try to relax."

I gritted my teeth as the horse took a wrong footing. I coughed with the pain and blood flew out of my mouth.

"Shit!"

As much as I had been in pleasure a few seconds ago with Sam and the others, it was now the exact opposite as I slumped over the horse in pain.

Noisulli calmed the horse. I think she was afraid he would buck us off. I think the smell of my blood and my coughing must have scared him. My vision was blurred and I tried to see where we were going. I could smell smoke and heard Noisulli calling out to someone. Then I was floating, but as I looked down I could see someone's legs, and I realized I was not floating but being carried. I figured it must be a man because I was no flyweight, and Noisulli would not have been able to carry me with such ease.

The voices were muffled as if I was listening to them underwater, and I could swear I could smell woodsmoke, and I thought maybe we were back in the cabin. Nothing really made any sense, and then I passed out again.

Chapter Twenty

"Wake up, Alex. Time to go." I opened my eyes, the pain was gone and I was back with Sam. I was relieved to be out of pain, and I felt my ribs just to make sure.

"You know I was back in my earth body again Sam, and I don't think by the way I was feeling that I am long for that world."

It felt strange to be talking like this. It was not that long ago that I thought I was going crazy and, come to think of it, very little time had passed since I didn't believe in any of this afterlife stuff.

"You will be OK, Alex. Your hardest decision is going to come when you have to make a choice to stay or go. The rest is just part of the process of you finding out who you are."

"So this is not normal, flitting between two worlds, or two realities?"

I was getting used to the fact that reality was only a point of perception, and I called heaven "world" only because it felt familiar and safe. The truth is I didn't really know what heaven was. Did I have a body in this place because I actually had one, or did I just perceive that I did?

"For most souls the process of what you would call crossing over, and what I would call being born, is usually straightforward. At first there is some confusion, but after a while things become clear, and the transition is smooth and painless. For some, though, like you, there is a choice to stay or crossover. These are usually souls that need to take a message back, and this is called a near-death experience.

"For these souls it can be hard to live in the physical world again, because they have tasted heaven. They usually have a compelling wish and desire to change the world, to bring love and healing. This can be hard for them, as those closest to them often don't believe their experience was real.

"They say things to them that imply it was just an hallucination, or the drugs the doctors gave them while they were unconscious. Many feel a compulsion to tell their story, but often it falls on deaf ears and they learn to become discerning about whom they talk to. Since a prophet is rarely accepted in his or her own land, they can also lose relationships and sometimes have to start again. This is the cross you have to bear when you touch heaven consciously, and it is one you, too, must carry if you decide to stay. The difference with you is your cross will be that much heavier, and there will be no one on earth to tell who you are. If you do they will just call you crazy, and ridicule you."

I thought about all the people in the past who had tried to say they had a message to give, and history taught me they were usually burnt at the stake or crucified.

"Not much of a choice then. Therefore, logic would dictate that I am better off staying here. Why would I want to help those who don't want my help? After all, the only thing I would get in return is abuse and them thinking I am crazy."

"The possibilities are endless, Alex. These are only two scenarios, but what you do and what you choose to experience is limitless."

"And if I decide to stay on earth, will I get to know Noisulli?"

"Again, that is up to you. I see you like her. Does this mean love is in the air?"

"No, especially as I might be about to croak it. Not the greatest start to a relationship. I was just hoping you could give me some inside information; it might give me some incentive to stay in my earth body."

"I think that's called insider trading, and highly illegal!"

"You are on your own on this one."

"Spoilsport!"

Chapter Twenty-One

We thanked Simon and Elizabeth for their hospitality, and I asked them to say goodbye to Peter from me. I felt a sense of sadness at leaving them, though I had only known them for such a short time. We had no need to carry anything with us, after all we were in heaven, which was something I was having a lot of trouble understanding and accepting. I expected heaven to be full of clouds and harps. Then again, I didn't believe in heaven until just recently, and any expectation of it was based on the Sunday school teachings I had received as a child.

Heaven was very real, though, and the rocks my feet would occasionally hit hurt just as much as if I was still in my earth body. This puzzled me and, since Sam was obviously my teacher and guide for this journey, I asked him why.

"You are a soul, Alex. You are a co-creator in your own reality. When God created you he ordained that you should have free will.

This means you have the choice to experience whatever you wish. Because you are still stuck between two worlds, you don't yet remember what potential you have within you. Your current experience of heaven is based on your perception of what is real to you in your earth life."

I was having a problem getting my head around the fact that I had two bodies, and I was existing simultaneously.

"So do you see what I see, in that case?"

"No, my perception is different from yours, but at this point in order to help you, I choose to experience heaven as you see it so that I can share your experience with you."

It was like trying to get a foothold while being in the centre of a tornado. I knew somewhere inside of me I understood and had the answers, but my software needed upgrading. I could not get through this veil before me. If only I could reach through I was sure I would understand everything.

"What is heaven really like, then?"

"Ah, now that's a question worth debating, one which has inspired painter and poet alike, has set brother against brother, and formed the basis of religion. Are you ready for the truth? Do you think, once you know, you can handle it?"

"I think if I can accept that I am in heaven, albeit my own perception, then, yes, I can accept the truth. Let's face it, everything I held to be true has been turned upside down. I think one more truth won't send me over the edge."

"OK, if you insist. Then here it comes. No one knows."

"Is that it? No one knows. That can't be right, someone must know."

"Yes, there is one being."

"What do you mean being? Is this an alien conspiracy?"

"God is a being and God knows what heaven is."

"Yes, I figured that one out for myself. What I meant, apart from God, does any one know what heaven is really like?"

"No."

"No one. Not one soul?"

"You see, I told you that you would not be able to accept the truth."

"So all those people in heaven are walking around seeing different things?"

"Yes."

"But when I was with you and Simon and Peter and Elizabeth we were all seeing the same things."

"Yes, but only because it served to make you feel more comfortable."

"I don't get it. There must, at some point, be a collective agreement as to what heaven is."

"There is the collective agreement. It is what you perceive heaven

WHEN THE STUDENT IS READY THE MASTER WILL APPEAR

to be is what heaven is, or did you think that free will stops when you leave your physical body? Free will was given before what you call the fall. How else do you think the fall happened? Do you think if souls did not have free will that they would have been able to be separate from God?"

"Well, that's going to upset a few people."

"No, not really, because in life they believe that heaven is a certain way, and when they pass over that is how they will see it. You see heaven as very physical and in many ways just like earth, but that is because you did not believe in heaven. Let me put it another way. Imagine God is a parent. Everyday he tries to guide his children in how things are, the difference between perceived right and wrong. Then one day the children grow up and leave home, and venture out into the world. They start to realize there is a big world out there, and it is far more complex than they first thought. They have experiences, good and bad, and begin to form their own opinions of the world. Then one day, while they are having a particularly bad day, they receive a phone call from their father. After discussing what's happening, the father says, 'Why don't you come home?' So the children return home. When they get home, one of the children says to their father, 'Why have you changed everything?' and the father replies,

'I have changed nothing. It is you who have changed; you are looking at things with a new perspective.' So you see God knows what heaven is, and always has done, and he knows nothing has changed.

"Now, some weeks pass by, and the children say to their father, 'Have you changed things again, because everything is as it was before we left home?' The father replies, 'No, it has always been this way, it's just you are now seeing it as it really is.' And the son says, 'You know, I never realized how beautiful it was.' You see, you are always in heaven, but you take it for granted. Only when you are parted from it, and then return, do you see it for what it really is. One day we will all return home, then, and only then, will we see heaven collectively the same."

Chapter Twenty-Two

"Hey, you there, what do you think you are doing?"

It took me by surprise. He just appeared out of nowhere, large as life and thundering towards us. His aggression was apparent and he was evidently angry with us for some reason. Another twist in my perception of heaven, I thought it was all love and enlightenment.

He was a thickset man with dark, black hair and balding on the top. It was as if every muscle in his face was screwed up. He was almost snarling like some kind of wild animal. The closer he got, the more aggressive he grew, but it was strange, because instead of just seeing his aggression it was as if I was feeling it. I shivered as though someone had just walked over my grave, and then the fear struck me.

"What are you doing on my land? Can't you read? No trespassing!"

I was so taken aback I am ashamed to say I let Sam step forward and take him on, after all, he was probably more used to this than me.

"We are sorry to have offended you. I assure you if we had seen the sign we would have gone another way."

"You must be blind then. I have a good mind to kick your sorry butts for being so stupid!"

Now maybe I was between lives, and maybe this was heaven but, like all people I have met in life, I had a point where I could not be pushed beyond. And if there was one thing that wound me up it was sheer pig ignorance and bad manners. Yes, I swore now and then, maybe too often, but this numskull had made a rash judgment, and whatever we said I could see he was spoiling for a fight. And so it was at this point I snapped, maybe it was the emotion of the last few days. All I know was the next minute I was standing in front of Sam.

"Look here you arrogant shit, you might be big and you might be tall, and you also might be the noisiest thing on two legs, but if you think you can just threaten us, and think we are going to hide away in some dark corner, then you had better think again!"

I might as well have hit him. He just stopped, mouth open wide, and stood there looking at me.

When he finally did say something it was calm and yet I felt tinged with a couple of pounds of sarcasm. He spoke now in a soft tone, but it was thickly sweet and it made the hairs on the back of my neck stand up.

"You have a brave student this time." His comment was directed at Sam, who now stepped slowly in front of me, placing himself between me and this aggressive oaf. Then softly he said to me.

"Step back, Alex, and do exactly as I say."

Boy, whatever you could say about heaven it wasn't boring and, though Sam's voice was calm, I knew there was something going on I didn't understand. I felt for the first time as though my very soul was in danger.

"It's been a while. I see you are still throwing your weight around," said Sam.

"Yes, a lot has passed since we last met. I didn't recognise you at first. If I had known it was you I would have used a different approach."

All the time they moved in circles around each other, but Sam made sure he kept himself between us, and at no point did they drop their gaze. It reminded me of a bullfight, one false move and it was over.

"Yes, I am sure you would have but, if you remember, last time that didn't work either."

"So who do you have there? He must be a worthy student, and brave or stupid to take me on."

"He has nothing to do with you. If you have a problem then it is I who you should be quarrelling with."

"On the contrary, they all are my concern, as well you know, but what intrigues me is the way you guard him. He must be a great prize."

I don't know what was happening, but I felt afraid and sick at the same time. This was heaven, people didn't fight. Was this my distorted perception of heaven again creating this situation? If so, I wanted it to stop, but nothing I could do would change the situation.

I tried to think of green fields and calm water, but still this arrogant man remained locked in combat with Sam.

Then, for a split second he caught my eye. It was as if my whole body froze and I was crippled with fear; I wanted to throw up.

Sam quickly stepped between us again.

"Don't look at him, Alex."

"Ah, so that's why you guard him so well. Finally the penny drops.

He looks a little different, but the eyes never change. I can see why you wouldn't want me to have this one. But then again I was never one to ask, I think I will just take him."

Again Sam made sure I was between them. "You forget who you are talking to," he said.

"You don't remember me do you, Alex, but you will, and trust me you will be glad to come with me. How can you be with him after what you did, or is it you don't remember?"

Remember what, I thought. Did everyone here know who I was except me?

"That's it! He hasn't told you who you are, has he? Now that's clever, even worthy of praise. The deceit, I love it, just imagine what he will do when he finds out. Shall I tell him?"

At that Sam raised his right hand above his head. I thought he was going to hit him but instead he shouted out loud, "Satanayuwta, leave now, you are not welcome in this house!"

Then before my eyes this aggressive man reacted as though he was in terrible pain. He might as well have been covered in boiling oil.

He fled as fast as he could, screaming obscenities as he went. I managed to catch Sam just in time as his legs gave way, and he fell to the floor.

"Are you OK?"

"Yes, I am fine. It just took more out of me than I thought."
"What was that all about? Do you know that guy?"
"Yes, we have met a few times before, but this time he was after you."
"What is it with this place? Why does everybody look at me like they do? And why was he after me? What the hell is so special about me?"
"I am afraid I can't tell you. When the time is right you will know."

I resigned myself to the fact that no one was going to tell me, but I still wanted to know who the aggressive stranger was.

"OK, so I accept I will have to wait to discover the great secret, but if you say I was a saint I will laugh in your face. Although I think I have a right to know who that guy was."

"Satan."

Sam stood up, dusted himself off, and started walking along the path as if nothing had happened.

"Wow! Hold on! Time out! You can't nonchalantly just drop a bombshell like that and walk off into the sunset. What do you mean, Satan?"

"Just that. Satan."

"What? The Satan?"

"Yes."

"And that gobbledegook stuff you said, which made him hightail it out of here? What was that?"

"Aramaic, an ancient language. I called him by his real name so he had no doubt that I knew who he was."

"So you're not kidding. That was really Satan, Lucifer, the man from down below."

"Yes, Alex. Is it so hard to comprehend?"

"No, I just don't see what he wanted with me. I mean, thanks for sticking up for me, but why me?"

"He is the great deceiver and when a soul passes over sometimes they don't know they are dead, or they can't accept it. At this point you could say they are vulnerable. As you did not believe in heaven you were one of these souls, and knowing this I was sent to get you and make sure you had safe passage."

"You know, I feel pretty stupid at this moment. I told Satan I was going to kick his sorry ass. He could have flattened me like a fly, right?"

"Yes, that was a bit stupid, but funny too, only because you did not know who he was."

"I thought he would have had horns and a long tail, or is that just a myth?"

"He shows himself in many ways, usually in the least expected. The trick is to be able to see through the disguise."

"And that language, what did you call it?"

"Aramaic."

"I take it he speaks it too?"

"Yes, and so do you. Oh, except you don't remember."

I felt like a puppet and everyone except me was pulling my strings.

I was just acting out the motions. It was like seeing a slow-motion punch and just standing there waiting for it to hit.

Chapter Twenty-Three

My head felt like it was going to explode and the headache was worse. The smell of smoke was getting stronger. I managed to open my eyes slightly and made out the figure of an old man sitting next to me. In one hand he was holding what looked like a bunch of small burning twigs, but it had a pungent sweet smell. And with his other hand he was wafting smoke over me with a feather. I was still finding it hard to stay conscious, but in my lucid moments I could hear the old man chanting in a low melodic voice. I was also aware of someone gently holding my hand, which I found warm and comforting. The pain in my ribs was now a dull throbbing ache, and the slightest movement would make me pass out again. The taste of blood in my mouth confused me, and I tried in vain to figure out what was going on. The more I tried the less clear it became; I was caught between two worlds, not knowing which one was the illusion. I was falling into a void of darkness, not knowing if I would suddenly land with a bump, or awaken to find that this was all a dream. Or was this a dream about a dream? All that was clear to me was that everything was unclear, and I had the sense that I was losing my grip on sanity.
"Shhhhhhh, Alex."
That was all I needed, that sound of reassurance, and once again I peacefully passed out.

Chapter Twenty-Four

Our encounter earlier had shaken me a bit, and I didn't really feel like talking. Until now I had felt safe, confused, but safe, and I longed for my old normal life.

My memory of the past was getting better, but I also knew that this meant I was not doing well in my physical body. I felt a sense of sadness at the prospect of leaving my earthly life behind, and couldn't help but wonder if I had wasted my time. There were things I was ashamed of doing, so I decided, there and then, if I did return to earth I would do everything in my power to rectify this. All the things I had worried about, what had that all been about? This was reality and if I could just remember this, I would never take a single thing for granted again. One thing was troubling me, though, which was more important, being incarnate or staying in heaven?

"Sam, is being in this place more important than being on earth?"

"No, both are equally important. There is an expression that says, 'Be careful of becoming so saintly that your earthly existence is no good.' There are many that have tried to reach spiritual enlightenment, and in the process have not seen what is before their eyes. The physical, as you call it, and the soul are one and the same. Do you think the body could exist without the soul? Many souls only discover this when they no longer live on earth and then, like the person who develops arthritis and wishes they had been more active, it is too late. As dark and light are defined by each other so is the body and the soul, so don't waste one day worrying because tomorrow it may be too late."

"So is it too late for me?"

"It is never too late to change."

"So what happens if you find it is too late. Does that mean that it's game over?"

"As I said, it is never too late."

"But you said tomorrow may be too late."

"Yes, but then there is always another day, no experience is wasted. What I am saying is stop worrying, enjoy the experience. You don't bite into a juicy orange and think, 'What if this is bad?' On the contrary you just bite it expecting it to be juicy and thirst quenching. The problem is, most of you have forgotten that if you expect something to happen it often does. If you could just treat your physical life like the orange, and expect it to be good, then you would stop worrying and trying to find the bad in everything."

"But we don't want it that way. It's just that sometimes that's how it turns out."

"Really? Is that so? If you could hear the thoughts of people everyday you might not be saying that. How often do you think people think, 'Oh well, another day, another dime, another dollar.' Is that embracing life? Is that enjoying the fruit of life? You should give thanks for each sacred moment of life in the physical body. Be joyful because the experience you have chosen is perfect. Give thanks for the life of your children and other wonderful opportunities to grow and learn."

"OK, I see your point, but surely it's not that simple? If it was, would all those on earth not be doing it right now?"

"That's the problem. It is that simple, and that is also why it is so complicated."

"I don't understand."

"If you walked down the street and started handing out money for free to people, do you think everyone would take it? No, because that would be too simple. They would be suspicious, or tell you where to go. If you all stopped being so afraid and saw how life could really be, the world could change in an instant."

"So if God loves us why doesn't he just send someone to sort the whole mess out?"

"He does and he has, but you were so afraid then, as you are now, that you crucified them, burnt them, or laughed at them. You expect the heavens to open, a shaft of light to descend and a host of angels to sing. You can't see the divinity in his messengers unless you have a light show with all the pyrotechnics. What does that say about your faith? Can you not see the bounty on earth? Look beyond your preconceived ideas, see what you have and see what you are given everyday. You are only limited by your ideas of your limitations."

"Surely it's not that simple?"

"And so be it, until you see how simple it is."

This felt like Sunday school on a grand scale, except this time I was old enough to disagree and ask more questions than I would have as a child. My emotions were up and down like a yo-yo, I felt like a young, pubescent teenager again. There were great moments of joy and excitement, followed by doubt and fear. It was as if I was fighting my own demons. I had, in an instant, seen the simplicity of life, and yet, at the same time, how complex it was. Some might say that I was lucky to have the choice to stay here in heaven or to return to earth, but thinking and talking about it is one thing, when you are actually faced with the reality of making the choice it's not that simple. At that moment I envied those that died and passed over without having to make a choice.

Chapter Twenty-Five

There was an intensity to the light and sounds in this place, everything was more pronounced, the colours were more vivid than on earth and, as much as I was starting to enjoy the journey, I was still impatient to find out what the big secret was.

Why did I have to take this journey? I knew that my perception of heaven and even my thoughts were the things that were creating my surroundings and making this all so familiar. So why could I not just change my thoughts and see the journey at its end, then the answer could unfold and I could move forward.

I was stubborn by nature and this had stopped me from seeking advice in the past, but in this place I was out of my depth, so unless I asked a question I was not going to get an answer. Sam only gave me answers if I made the first move, and I knew if I wanted to get to the bottom of this mystery I would have to put pride and stubbornness aside.

I just had to go ahead and keep questioning, so I asked him why I couldn't just see the end of the journey now.

"It's a question of enlightenment, Alex. Taken literally it means light where there was once dark."

"Yes, but would it not be enlightening for me to ask you for the answer and have you give it to me?"

"Let me tell you about a man who thought the same way as you and maybe you will see why I can't do this. There was a man once who, throughout his youth, had studied books on spiritual matters hoping to attain some sort of secret knowledge. Unfortunately, he found all the books he read, though called different things, basically gave the same answer. Then one day he came across a book with a title that really caught his eye, and he thought to himself, 'Finally, the answer I have been looking for.' But like you he wanted, after all this time, to have the answers sooner than later. So instead of reading each section, and taking time to follow the instructions and exercises and master the lessons, he turned to the last chapter and followed the instruction.

"The next day he woke up after a restless night's sleep feeling sick.

As each day passed he became worse, so finally a priest was called, as his parents were so worried he might not make it.

"The doctors were baffled as to why he had become so ill so quickly. Now this priest was wise and experienced, and knew that the matters of the soul were just as valid as the matters of the body, and how one affected the other. He noticed the book at the side of the young man's bed and, suspecting what may have happened, he asked the young man if he would be willing to be hypnotised. At this point his illness was so bad that he would have agreed to anything. So the priest hypnotised him and, while under hypnosis, suggested that he forget everything he had read in the last chapter of the book. He then brought the young man around, who, in the next hour, much to the amazement of the doctors, returned to almost full health.

The priest then told him, "In a few days when you are feeling strong again come and see me."

But before the priest left, he took the book with him. So following the priest's request, after a few days had passed, the young man went to see him.

Now, obviously the young man's first question was, 'Why did I become so ill?' and the priest, instead of giving him the answer, tore the first page out of the book handing it to the young man saying,

'Here, go and read and study this and come back and see me in a year.'

"You see, Alex, just because you can't see it, taste it, or hear it, rather like faith, it does not mean it is not real. Enlightenment, like anything, comes when you are willing to be patient. If it's going to last it's not going to be through taking short cuts.

WHEN THE STUDENT IS READY THE MASTER WILL APPEAR

"So be patient and accept that all will become clear in the right moment and the right time."

"Is that why you sent Satan on his way before he could spill the beans?"

"Yes, and also because I knew you didn't have the knowledge yet to beat him."

Finally, I had to agree, and saw that there was only one way through this and that meant doing something I was not very good at, being patient.

Chapter Twenty-Six

In the haste of life on earth there is often very little time to think, as everyone is so busy doing. Here in heaven, though, I had plenty of time, because time didn't exist. Walking towards a destination without the knowledge as to when you will arrive tended to concentrate the mind. This, of course, was assuming I had a mind.

You were also free of worldly worries like money, shelter and food. This was taking me a while to get used to. I was beginning to understand the sanctity of food, something I had taken for granted on earth. I was also getting my head around the fact that thoughts were also just as real, and if I concentrated on them with the right intent, they could and would shape my reality and perception of my surroundings and experiences. The trick appeared to be the ability to control your thoughts as easily as you controlled your speech and action.

This was no easy thing to do, and just when I thought I had mastered it, some random thought would hit me, usually something very trivial, but nonetheless enough to destroy my concentration. As we walked I tried over and over to hold only one thought in my mind without being sidetracked. I found that if you could try and ignore your other senses, and focus only on your thoughts, it was easier.

I was determined to master this skill by the time we reached wherever it was we were heading.

Maybe I had bitten off more than I could chew. I was still trying to get to the end of the book without reading the first page.

The difference was that here you were not limited by the physical. However, there were a whole new set of challenges. For instance when you thought of something and you wanted to make it appear, just like a sculpture, you had to see it from every angle or you would end up with a one-dimensional object. And, as if this was not hard enough, the dimensions were limitless. Forget one and two dimensions, according to Sam when you became practiced you could make objects move.

I was nowhere near this point of proficiency, and just holding a thought long enough in my head without it being bushwhacked by another thought was hard enough. So we walked on and I kept practising. It was strange because this made me quite tired, which surprised me, after all I was only thinking and I no longer had a dense physical earth body to contend with.

"You know, Sam, I am so tired. Is this normal? Surely if we don't need food then we also don't need sleep?"

"You still need, and are using, energy, but now you don't have to get this from food. The more you progress, the finer your body will become, and the less you will need dense physical matter to survive. Heaven is endless, as the illusion of time is endless. This part of heaven you are now in, though finer in density than earth, is still very dense in comparison to other dimensions within heaven. In this place, manifesting thought takes as much energy as physical labour on earth."

"OK, I can accept that, but do I need to sleep? Is there any way around this? I have never seen you sleep in all the time we have been here."

"Yes, but before I teach you this you need to understand something about how energy works."

"Is this going to be a complicated physics lesson?"

"No, but if you want me to make it complicated I can."

"No, it's OK. Keep it simple, please, physics was never my strong point."

"Energy is limitless and perpetual, it never dies. Though it may come to an end this does not mean that it is no longer there, it just means it has taken on new form."

"You see I am lost already."

"OK. Think of it this way. A weight suspended by a piece of

string in the air is what you would call kinetic energy. It is energy with potential. If you cut the string the weight would fall. This weight could be attached to a pulley system and a generator wheel. This would turn the wheel and the result would be electricity. So the energy was always there, stored as potential energy, just waiting to be released. Now everything has energy and the only thing that separates this is the speed at which it vibrates. The slower the energy vibrates the denser the object, the faster it vibrates the lighter and more pliable the object. Are you still with me?"

"Yes, believe it not, so far all is clear."

"Good. Now, when that energy is released like the kinetic energy, it is spent, or so you would think but, in fact, that energy is transformed. It is like saying when you boil a kettle and change water into steam then the water no longer exists, but that's not true. In fact, when the steam cools, it once again becomes water."

"So how do we make the jump from this to sleep?"

"Sleep in heaven, as you like to call it, is all to do with energy, as it is on earth. On earth you think that you need sleep so that the body can rest and repair itself, but if this is the case why is that some people need more sleep than others?"

"Maybe it's because their work is more labour intensive and therefore they need more time to replace it."

"But what are they replacing?"

"Energy, of course."

"Yes, and where does this energy come from?"

"Food."

"So if this is true then why sleep, why not just eat more?"

"I never thought of that. So where does the energy come from?"

"Each person, depending on his or her own emotional state, requires less or more energy. Have you noticed when you are feeling particularly emotional about something, yet have done very little, how tired you feel? This is because emotions and the soul are very closely connected. The soul vibrates at a very fast rate so fast that it cannot be seen with your physical eyes. Emotion also vibrates at a very fast rate, but when you experience anger or grief this vibration slows down. When this happens, the link between the soul and body becomes harder to maintain."

"So are you saying that energy is emotional? Does this mean, then, that all energy is emotional?"

"No. I am saying that what you think of as energy on earth is only one aspect in a very dense, slow form. You will notice that the more advanced a culture becomes the more they discover finer, faster and efficient forms of energy. For example, it was not that long ago you relied on, and burnt, fossil fuels in your homes, but now you have nuclear power. As your civilization progresses, and if it gets past this critical phase in its development without destroying itself, you will discover faster, cleaner and more efficient energy."

"Right. Well, so far I can see what you are saying, but I am not emotional everyday."

"Really?"

"Yes, some days I feel great."

"And feeling great is not an emotion?"

"Yes, but it's not a negative emotion."

"And on those days have you noticed how you need less sleep, and when you do sleep you sleep better?"

"Checkmate. I get it, but we can't go around feeling good all the time."

"OK, I could see why you might think this, but do you think this will always be the case?"

"No, but currently our life is too stressful. I can see in the future, when we get past our current phase of evolution, there might come a time when our technology becomes more and more advanced, and we have less stress because things will be easier."

"So you think you will experience less, what you call, negative emotion and stress if you have better technology. So why is it that some of the poorest and most simple people on your earth are also the happiest? Emotion, be it positive or negative, constructive or destructive, is not based on material possession. It is precisely this belief that has got you into the mess you are today. You think that having more makes you happy."

"So how do we live in a constant state of positive emotion?"

"First, see that no emotion is negative or positive, but that one simply defines the other as day defines night. You would not say that the night is bad and the day is good. In doing this all emotion becomes positive."

"But anger is not a good feeling, and when people get angry they are often destructive."

"Yes, you are right, but if you live in a society where it was OK to feel angry and express this, then it need not become physical and destructive. It is only destructive because it is suppressed and, like anything under pressure, it is only a matter of time before it will blow."

"We are so far from this point, though. I would love to think we could be like this but I just can't see it."

"And therein lies your answer; your world is very young in the grand scheme of things. Like a child it learns and experiences, often through pain and suffering, but there will come a time when you no longer need to feel pain, because you will remember and in remembering will begin to see there is another way."

"I just realized that this whole conversation started because we were talking about sleep. I love the way that happens."

"Yes, like life, you start out in one direction and then end up in another, but in the end you always return to the point you started. So to return to that point and the answer to your original question, do you need to sleep and why I do not need to sleep? You will not need to sleep when your emotional body vibrates at the same speed as your soul. This does not mean you do not require rest, but when you rest you remain conscious, and in this state you are aware of the wonder of your physical body, and it takes very little to maintain it.

"I do not mean to run you down or imply you are a backward society, I am just stating things as I see them. At the moment you often treat your bodies with very little respect. Five minutes of conscious reflection will do more than eight hours of sleep."

"Is there a way to do this? Do I just close my eyes and breathe, or is it more complicated than this?"

WHEN THE STUDENT IS READY THE MASTER WILL APPEAR

Sam laughed at this point. For some reason I had said something that he found amusing and, without knowing what, I laughed as well.

"So what's so funny, what are we laughing about?"

"The fact that you think everything has to be complicated to have any worth. It is the simplest things that are often the hardest.

Has it not been said, 'Love your neighbour as you would yourself?' It's such a simple truth, no books to read, no exams to take, but can you do it? I will tell you how simple it is. Close your eyes, focus on your breathing, and think of nothing else but your body. Now, marvel at the wonder of this creation. When you can do this you can do anything, including loving your neighbour. When you see what a miracle of creation you are, you will also see what a miracle of creation your neighbour is."

"Wow, and all I wanted to know was why you don't need sleep. It's a good job I didn't ask you why there were so many flavours of ice cream."

And then we laughed, not just a little laugh but a belly, side-splitting laugh and I felt great. That night I didn't sleep and in the morning I closed my eyes and focused on my breathing, and rediscovered something I had first discovered as a child. I had this thing called a body, and it was truly a miracle of creation.

Chapter Twenty-Seven

The morning light in heaven was like no other light I had seen on earth. The only way I can describe it was to say it was clean and sharp, like the light that reflects off a crystal. Now and then you would see a shaft of light full of rainbow colours darting across the sky. It was as if the light was a living entity, and I felt that if I really concentrated hard enough I could feel it.

I remember as a child lying in bed transfixed by the light dancing on the ceiling. It was shining through a crystal prism my mother had hung in the window. When you are child things like that are magical and each day is a new adventure, full of wonderful discoveries.

So here I was once again, transfixed by the light, lost in the simple wonder of dancing patterns.

As I lay there looking up it dawned on me that I was becoming attached to this place, and I realized that it was not going to be that easy when the time came to make the decision to stay here or to return to my earth body. I also began to experience memories that were very real, but it was as if they were not my memories and yet they were. This made me feel a little uneasy.

Sam was sitting under an olive tree staring off into the distance. I looked up to see what he was staring at, but there was nothing I could see in front of him that appeared to be of any interest. I thought he must have been daydreaming.

"Sam."

"One second, I will be with you in a moment. Let me just finish this conversation."

I looked around expecting to see someone but, unless they were invisible, I couldn't see or hear anyone. But I gave him the benefit of the doubt, after all this was heaven and a lot of things I once thought to be true were now falling away from my past reality. I sat in silence waiting for him to finish his conversation with someone who wasn't there.

"OK, Alex, I am all ears. What did you want to know?"

"Well, I do have a question, but first can you tell me who you were talking to? Unless I have had too much sun, I didn't see anyone."

"Do you remember we talked about vibration and how some things vibrate at different speeds? The slower they vibrate the denser they become, and the faster they vibrate the lighter and finer they become."

"Yes."

"Well, I was talking to a soul who was vibrating at a higher level and this is why you couldn't see her."

"But why couldn't I hear her then?"

"When your soul body starts to vibrate at a faster level then communication using sound also becomes unnecessary. At this level all communication is by thought."

"That must feel really weird."

"Imagine a speaker inside your head, except instead of sound you get pictures. You have heard the expression a picture paints a thousand words. Well, that saying is true. When you communicate this way, a conversation that would normally last for hours, can take seconds. You could talk about the history of the earth from start to finish in an hour."

"I guess you have to be very careful what you picture then."

"Yes, but with practice this becomes easier. It's like learning sign language. At first it's awkward but the better you get the faster and more accurate you become. Eventually you forget you communicated in any other way."

"So what happens if someone starts talking using sound to someone who uses thought?"

"Believe it or not, this happens all the time on earth."

"It does? I have never come across it, and believe me I think I would remember."

"If someone who communicates using thought to someone who uses sound, it is like tuning into a radio station. At first you get a lot of crackling then bit by bit you find the right frequency. On earth you have had people since the start of your time who have been able to do this. They have been called prophets and some call them saints.

A good example of this was a young girl called Joan of Arc. She caused quite a stir in her day and, like most prophets, they are seldom accepted in their own town or even country. So when she no longer served a purpose and people became afraid of her, she went the way of many of God's messengers, and was burnt at the stake."

"Yes, I have always felt sad for her. These days on earth at least you can be as mad as you like without being burnt to death for it."

"I wouldn't be so sure, Alex. Your modern history, just like your old history, is full of people of peace that accomplish great things with love, and as a consequence meet a sticky end."

"I don't know any one who was burnt at the stake in my lifetime."

"No, but they are shot, tortured and ridiculed, just because they are different and try to show us there is another way to do things."

"Two that you will know well were Martin Luther King and John F Kennedy."

"Yes, but we also had Mother Teresa and no one tried to kill her."

"That's because she did not upset the status quo, and was non-political, whereas Dr King and Kennedy changed things by challenging the political establishment head on. This ruffled quite a few feathers."

"Will we ever change and start listening to these messengers then?"

"Yes, slowly and surely you are getting the message. It's been over two thousand years since you crucified one of the greatest messengers, and still you refuse to listen. As time passes they leave their mark and, like a giant jigsaw, the pieces start to fall into place, until you can no longer deny the truth because it is staring you straight in the face."

"You know, before we started talking about this there was something else I wanted to ask you, because it has been troubling me."

WHEN THE STUDENT IS READY THE MASTER WILL APPEAR

"And what was that?"

"As I spend more time here with you, I appear to be having these memories, but they don't feel like they belong to me. I see faces and places I don't recognise but feel that I should."

"This is normal and you are not going mad, and you are right, you should recognise these places and faces because these are your memories from your past when you first stepped into the cosmos."

"But I don't remember the people or places so how can they be mine?"

"When a soul decides to incarnate they also choose to forget what they were, and what they know. When they return to heaven they start to remember. In your case this is slow as you still may choose to return to your earth body."

"But why forget at all? I don't see the point in this."

"Imagine seeing a sunflower for the first time, or holding your first child. This is a magical experience, which can only be experienced in the same way once. After this, although the experience is still a great pleasure, it never has that same intensity. So each soul chooses to forget, because they know this is the only way they can really have and experience this feeling as if it was the first time."

"But what about the negative feelings and experiences? Why would one want to experience these?"

"Again, Alex, it comes down to your perception of what is negative and what is positive. If each experience is helping you to grow then there is no such thing as a negative experience."

"So will I remember who these people are, and where these places are?"

"Yes, but not until you first discover who you are. I know this is hard for you at the moment, and I keep saying this, but you really are in a special position of being able to make a conscious choice as to whether you stay here or return to earth."

"And when I discover who I am, will I remember this on earth?"

"Yes, but, as I have said before, no one will believe you, and at this point you may not want to return to earth."

"I guess that is a decision I will have to make when this whole thing becomes clear. I just hope I am someone I like. If I find out I was Adolf Hitler it would have been better to let our angry friend take me away."

"Don't worry, you were not Adolf Hitler, but that would have been an interesting dilemma."

I knew he was joking, but I was also unsure what he would have done if faced with this dilemma. I pitied the soul who has to deal with that scenario.

Chapter Twenty-Eight

At times I felt like a child in a candy store, except in this case I didn't have an adult telling me not too eat too much. I was hungry for knowledge, and if I did decide to return to my life on earth and not have people accept or believe what had happened to me, I might as well make the most of it and find the answers to all those questions you never get the answers to.

As my memories returned I knew that my track record on relationships was pretty shoddy. It was not for want of trying though. Getting a girl was the easy bit, but keeping her? Now, that was another thing.

Here I was with the chance to find out where I had gone wrong. Was there some secret formula to keeping a woman? Would I finally have the answer and discover where I was going wrong?

"Sam, I know you will have been asked this a thousand, if not a million, times before: what is the secret to a good relationship? Why do so many marriages fail theses days?"

"It might surprise you to know that I am seldom asked that question, as most souls who pass over are not caught between two planes of existence. They remember, as their vibration changes, and know all the answers in a second. In your case things are on hold. However, I did promise to answer all but two questions, so I will tell you."

I was looking forward to this. If I decided to return then maybe, finally, I could have a loving, lasting relationship. I might even write a book about it.

"When two people get together you think this is some random event. Alternatively, you don't have a relationship, in the vain hope that the only person worth having a relationship with is what you call your soulmate."

"Is this so tragic? Surely it is better to spend your life with one right person than many wrong ones?"

"That's my point. There are no wrong ones, and often the person who you react to the most is, in fact, your soulmate. To suggest that any relationship, be it friendship or love, is a game of chance, is to say that a flower may or may not open on a sunny day. There is an order to the universe, and this also applies to relationships. They are not some random event, but calculated, agreed upon interactions to advance and develop your soul."

"So you are saying that even a destructive relationship is good?"

"I am saying that it is only destructive if viewed within the limited context of your current understanding."

"But that's just a cop out! What about all the harm that it does?"

"Tell me. If you had nothing bad, as you say, happen to you in life. If everything happened as you wanted it to. If you never fell over as a child or experienced loss, do you think you would be who you are today?"

"No, because I am the sum of my experiences."

"Exactly, and do you think a soul created by God with free will would not have the ability to experience and choose its experiences?"

"But why would anyone choose to have destructive, failed relationships?"

"Good question, and the answer is a bit like noughts and crosses, or what you might call tic-tack-toe. It is only when you have exhausted all the possibilities that you realize that no one can win this game.

So you come to the only solution possible, don't play the game.

Life is a game and you have many possibilities but, ultimately, you return to one answer, which is that you are an indestructible, divine soul playing an elaborate game."

"But why play the game in the first place?"

"In order to answer that question I will first have to tell you some history, and I don't mean the history you learnt in school, this is the history of creation."

"Do you mean Charles Darwin and the theory of evolution? I know all about that."

"No, this is the history of the creation of the soul, and you can't carbon date and give it a time. This is a timeless history, and it started before time was even thought of as a concept.

"There was a time when God was alone and all that he knew was himself. There were no planets, there was no light, and there was no dark. Essentially, you could say he was lonely. Now, as you know from Sunday school, he started to create the universe as we know it today. But still God was alone, so he created souls and he loved them and nurtured them. There was nothing the souls wanted, for they experienced no pain, hunger or suffering. They were surrounded by, and fed on, the love from God. It was a symbiotic relationship, each learning from the other. Then one day one of the souls thought things should be different, and that God should not be calling all the shots. "This soul was called Lucifer, and he started spreading discontent throughout God's house. Soon there was a split, and souls started taking sides. This was the first war ever and God's heart was full of sadness. He cast Lucifer and his followers into the earth, in an attempt to remove the rotten apples form the barrel before they contaminated the whole of heaven. But God was, and is, a loving God, so he also seeded the earth with good fruit, in the belief that this would one day return things to a point of balance. Lucifer, from that day, has been at war with God, and the game of life started.

"Whatever God did, Lucifer would try to mimic, but God has a weapon that is more powerful than anything Lucifer has, and Lucifer knows this. So he tries to use hate, pain and suffering to maintain the divide. This has backfired on him, because even when man experiences pain and suffering the soul still grows and develops in leaps and bounds."

"What is the weapon that God has? I don't remember that one in Sunday school."

"Love."

"Love? How can love be a weapon?"

"Love is the fabric of the universe, and when you see that God is a forgiving God, and that even those souls that sided with Lucifer can be forgiven and return home, then love becomes a powerful weapon, and Lucifer can do nothing to counteract this."

"Then why does he still try? If I knew that my enemy had a powerful weapon that I could do nothing about, the most logical course for self-preservation would be to wave the white flag and surrender."

"That assumption is based on logic, but this is not logic. The point of this history lesson is to teach you that this is rather like playing a game of chess, albeit a very long and elaborate one, in which one move can take millions of years. Like chess, just when you think you are winning, your opponent can suddenly put you into check."

"So are you saying then that Lucifer can still win?"

"I don't even know the answer to this question, Alex, but I can tell you he has not yet been able to destroy love. As long as there is one person alive who is willing to love, no matter what might be done to him or her, then the game goes on."

"So how does this relate to relationships and the secret to having a good relationship that lasts?"

"By being aware of the game, Alex. By seeing that a relationship is not a coincidence of random people bumping into each other.

"Although you might feel anger and pain at times, you don't have to play Lucifer's game. You can be the master of your own game; God has given us all the pieces. How you place them and move them on the chessboard that you call life is up to you. So when you perceive that someone has hurt you or you have a failed relationship, stand back from the board and see it in the greater context of all the other pieces. You might even see that the last move you made has, in fact, put you in a stronger position, and brought you closer to checkmate."

"Boy, they are going to love this if I go back. When they ask me the secret to a loving, lasting relationship and I say chess, I am telling you now, I will get some funny looks!"

Chapter Twenty-Nine

I collected firewood while Sam built the fire for the night. Why we needed a fire was as strange as why we should need food, but the fire was comforting, as was the food, and I was grateful for this.

They reminded me of my life on earth, and also that I still had the possibility to return there.

We settled for the night as the moon rose and the stars burst into life. There is something mesmerising about a fire, it has a way of drawing you in and sending you deep into contemplation. It was while staring into the fire that I started thinking about the times in my life when I had learned so much. Usually this was accompanied by moments of great pain, and even suffering.

"You look deep in thought, Alex."

"Yes, I was just thinking about the time I was ill and had to go to hospital. It was a turning point in my life."

"Yes, illness can be a great teacher if we let it, but most people fight it."

"I remember fighting it. Only at the point that I was hospitalized did I give in. I realized that I wasn't going anywhere, and I might as well accept that I was here to stay for the foreseeable future."

"And what did you learn?"

"Well, that's the strange thing. I was in a ward with five other guys, all old enough to be my grandfather, and it dawned on me that no matter what we do in life, and no matter how rich we are, we all end up in the same place."

"Was this the first time you realized this?"

"No, not really, but it was the first time it was a reality for me, because here I was in hospital, and all that separated me from the others was my age. All of a sudden, all the stress and anxiety that had been partly responsible for me being ill was gone. From that moment on I decided to live each day to the full, and let the past and tomorrow be just that. I couldn't change them so I might as well start living in the moment.

"Sam, have you ever spent time in hospital?"

"No, not hospital, but there were times I also suffered and, like you, I prayed to God for help."

I could imagine Sam on earth. I thought he must have been a farmer or something like that, because judging by his build he was used to doing physical work. Then again, he had a calming influence and could have been a counsellor.

"Sam, what did you do on earth? Were you a teacher like Elizabeth said, and what caused you so much pain?"

"Yes, believe it or not, I was a teacher, also a bit of a radical. This got me into trouble now and then, but it was worth it. Sometimes you have to take great risks to achieve great things, and if you want to inspire people you have to make them think."

"So did you also get ill?"

"Not in the same way as you but, yes, you could say I got ill. More an illness of the heart, though, because of all the destruction and hate I saw around me."

"And did you also learn a lot from your moments of pain?"

"Yes, more than I ever realized, and in that moment of my greatest suffering, I understood that people are not bad, they just don't understand what it is they do. If they did they would stop doing it. Some people say that people are bad, that they are sinners, but it is only a sin when you do something that you know beforehand is a sin and still do it."

"So are you saying that it is OK to murder someone as long as you didn't know it was bad when you did it?"

"No, because there is a difference between what we all, in our hearts, know is a sin, no matter how we try to camouflage it. And once you strip the layers down as to why people would kill someone, the seed of truth is that it is wrong to take a person's life. It's strange.

WHEN THE STUDENT IS READY THE MASTER WILL APPEAR

I've had this conversation with others that have taken this journey, and you all at some point get around to the question of what is right and what is wrong. You all bring up the question of murder, but if we take some basic rules that you on earth live by, it is the simplest rule that after thousands of years you still have trouble with."

"I don't understand. What rules?"

"Well let's take what you call your ten commandments. One of the rules is that you should not kill. Now, as I said, we know in our hearts that this is true, but you also have another rule, which says love your neighbour as you would yourself. In comparison to not murdering you would think this was an easy rule to follow, but this is not the case because, as it says, you also have to love yourself.

"Loving yourself is not easy for the majority of people. How many people do you know who can actually say they do this? They usually think they are sinners beyond saving, and the hate they feel for themselves is more than anyone else could ever have towards them. They say things like, 'I am not good enough,' 'He or she is better than me.' Do you know if you followed this simple rule you would see that it would be impossible to murder anyone, because how could you murder a person you loved as much as yourself? You see, if you hate yourself then it easy to murder others."

"But what about those who are sent to war? They don't have a choice."

"No, Alex, there is always a choice. If every man and woman followed this simple rule no one would go to war. We would stop being afraid of each other, and it's fear that starts wars. It is fear of loving yourself and thinking you are not worthy that separates you from God."

"What did you teach when you were on earth?"

"What I am teaching you now. I tried to set people free from their bonds, but sometimes it takes time for an idea to come of age.

"Many have since tried to pass on the same message, often being killed in the process. Like a great oak, though, each year its bark becomes thicker and thicker until eventually it stands strong, able to weather any storm. In this case, the message, like the tree, is strong, and is able to stand as a great truth. Lucifer would like to take an axe and cut it down, but unless he can turn you all against each other, and as long as there is one left who will still love his neighbour as he would himself, then no matter what happens the axe will always remain blunt, and the truth will never be destroyed."

"Is this what is meant when someone says they have faith then?"

"When people talk of faith, I see that the way they say it is often like they say, 'Of course I have a car,' as if it something they expect all people to have, just like another commodity.

"What they don't see is that faith is not a religion, or a set of dogmatic rules, faith is a knowing that comes from deep within. It almost can't be quantified or explained. So when I say to someone, 'Why do you believe what you believe?' if they can't explain it and just say I do, I just feel it, don't ask me why, then I know they get it. However, if they feel the need to justify it and get angry that you would dare to question them, I know then they still are searching and questioning if they really believe it."

Chapter Thirty

As we sat by the fire I felt like I was on a roll, one question led to another, I wanted to know everything. Sparks flew into the air, brilliant and radiant red against a backdrop of a pitch-black night, studded with stars. It was hard to contain my energy. The more I discovered the more I wanted to know.

"The big question I have, then, is what happens to great people in the world who have done wonderful things in the name of peace, yet come from a different religion? Do they also go to heaven?"

"It is written in one of your great books that there are many rooms in God's house, and it is also written that as you judge so shall you be judged. It is not the place of man to judge his neighbour. For if you say that this man, or this woman, is not as good as you, then truly I say to you, it is right that the log in your eye has blinded you when your brother's eye has only a splinter."

I knew what Sam meant, but it still left the question that had always puzzled me, the debate about which religion was right.

"Sam, I understand what you are saying, but each religion on earth says they have the answer, and because of this they look down on those who would not follow their way. They say things like, 'You will go to hell,' or, 'This is the only way.'"

"And it's because of this you have burnt and killed God's messengers and teachers. Let me tell you a campfire story as we are sitting by the fire, it might help to explain what I mean.

"There once was a woman travelling down a road. She had arranged to meet an old friend of hers for lunch. They had not seen each other for some years, and they thought it would be good to catch up on all the latest news. The problem was that when her friend had given her directions the phone line had been bad, and she had only managed to get very sketchy instructions. So after some while turning this way and that without any luck, she decided to stop and ask a passer-by for some help. 'Oh yes,' said the man, 'I know the place. Take the A264 then turn right at the second junction. After about a mile you will come to a fork in the road, at this take the left turning, then after about three quarters of a mile you will be there.'

"The woman thanked the man and set off, but after a while she thought, 'Was that right or left at the junction?' So, lost again, she stopped and asked a woman who was walking her dog if she could help her. The woman said, 'Certainly I know that place. Follow this road until you get to the Old Bull pub and then take a right. After about a mile you will come to the Duck and Hound pub, go left there and after about a mile you will be there.' She thanked the woman and once again set off, turning right when she got to the Old Bull pub.

"Then she thought to herself, 'Was that left or right at the Duck and Hound?'

"So once again she stopped and asked a passer-by for directions.

"'Yes.' said the man and he asked her for a piece of paper. The woman gladly obliged, and the man wrote down the directions.

"Eventually the woman found the place, and her old friend, and had lunch and caught up on all the latest news.

"You see, we are all like the woman asking for help and directions from different people. They all knew how to get there but had different directions. This does not mean one was right and one was wrong, but also, like the last person who helped the woman, there is a faster way to get somewhere when you are lost. So next time when you think of great teachers, and lovers of peace like Mahatma Gandhi, for example, and other messengers that God has sent, don't burn them at the stake or shoot them."

Once again I stared into the fire, memorised by the dancing flames, as Sam's words played around in my mind.

Chapter Thirty-One

The further we travelled the more the memories of the surrounding countryside started coming back to me. There were points when I even knew which way to go, and without knowing it I would sometimes be walking in front of Sam, as if I was the one showing him the way.

It was only when I turned to talk to him that I realized he was behind me and that I had been leading the way.

The smell of the warm air as it blew through the olive trees was comforting and familiar. I had adjusted to the heat now and could go for longer periods of time without getting so thirsty or feeling tired.

All the time, at the back of my mind, I knew that this was not real; it was only a projection of my mind and its preconceived idea of a time and space. I felt a familiarity about this place, albeit I had no conscious memories of it. However, the memories were becoming clearer as the days went by. That in itself was even an illusion because, according what Sam had taught me, there was no such thing as time. It, therefore, stood to reason that days did not exist either, but rather there was just one continuous moment that went on forever.

I didn't even know if Sam was real, or if, in fact, this whole thing was as I had thought before, just a very elaborate dream. I still had not mastered the separation from the idea that I did not need food or sleep. I did appear to need less of both now. And if what Sam was saying was true, and I had no reason to doubt him so far, if I decided to leave my earth body and return to this place I called heaven, then, and only then, did I feel I would not need the things I had needed on earth, such as food and sleep. For now, though, the need for sleep and food was a constant reminder of the choice I had. Without this, I am sure I would have easily forgotten my earth life, and settled into my new home. This was becoming more comfortable and familiar with every passing day.

The first sign of impending pain did not come as I fell or stumbled on a sharp rock, but rather a subtle change in the air temperature and a gust of wind. I looked up, and moving towards us was a black rain cloud, with sheets of rain hitting the distant hills. It was moving towards us with incredible speed, and I knew that unless we got under cover we would soon be soaked to the bone. At the time, it didn't occur to me that it was somewhat out of place, but nonetheless it was raining in heaven. If I had taken time to think about it, I would have realized that this had to be someone's thought projections. What I had failed to grasp, though, was that my own thoughts could be creating this.

Then it started. First came the lightning, it was biblical. The heavens opened as a bolt of lightening hit a tree with crack like a thousand whips, instantly turning the tree into a fireball.

The sound was like a bomb exploding, and in sheer terror I ran for cover. At least that was the idea, because, unfortunately for me, there was no cover. So in desperation I turned to Sam for help, somehow expecting an answer, but he was nowhere to be seen. Great! My guide, the man I had developed an instinctive trust for over the last few days, had deserted me in my hour of need.

I was soaked to the skin. I couldn't believe how fast this storm had hit us. Was this another lesson?

"Alex." At first it sounded like it was miles away, off in the distance. "Alex. Over here." This time it sounded closer. I peered through the rain, which by this time was coming down with such ferocity it was hard to see anything. I could just make out a dark shape of something. I couldn't tell if it was a tree or a large rock.

"Alex. Over here." It was Sam. His voice was muffled by the sound of the thunder and lightning. I followed his voice. Then a hand reached out of nowhere and grabbed me, pulling me into the shelter of a cave. I was wet and bewildered but glad to be out of the rain.

"I thought you had left me."

WHEN THE STUDENT IS READY THE MASTER WILL APPEAR

"No, I was calling you, but you couldn't hear me."
"What's happening?"
"It's a storm."
"No shit, Sherlock. I can see it's a storm, but this is heaven, paradise, you know, eternal sunshine. Have I done something to offend God? Please don't to tell me this is down to me."
"Guess it must be."
"What do you mean guess? Don't you know?"
"Only you and God know what is in your heart, Alex."
"Well, it's not a bloody thunderstorm of biblical proportions, that's for sure."
"You can only project what you know. Something must have happened for you to cause this storm. What were you thinking just before you saw the storm coming?"
"Nothing. I was just looking at a tree that was all knotted and twisted. I thought it was strange as all the trees around it were normal and perfectly formed. Then I noticed the storm. One minute it was in the distance, and the next, wham! I was running for cover, dodging lightening bolts."

The pain was like nothing I have ever experienced before. It was more painful than falling into the stream and breaking my ribs when I was with Noisulli. The pain dropped me to my knees, and my body felt like it was on fire. I felt as though I was falling through space, frantically trying to hold on to something in a vain attempt to halt my descent into a place I had to go, yet, in truth, would rather not.

They say that a midlife crisis is a life relived, but with the conscious chance to take control and steer your destiny. Up until this point my life had been a series of events that had happened to me, but now I was in pain and falling towards the chance to change all that. As with all experience, though, I did not know this at the time. My companion was no longer by my side. I was, for the first time in my life, alone and disconnected from everything. If I were to survive this I would need to somehow find a hidden strength inside me. One moment I was in the rain, and now this complete darkness.

The physical pain had gone, but what was left was worse. Before

I could have said I was never alone, because even though I professed not to believe in anything, in reality I kept a little corner of my mind for God. It was rather like carrying a survival kit for insurance, you never know when it may come in handy. Now, though, even that was gone. It was as if my lifeline and all that defined me as a human being was lost. Even my awareness of God being greater than everything no longer existed. And I was faced with one question, who am I?

It's not something we often ask ourselves. Yes, you are a mother, a father, a train driver, a nurse, but that's what you do it's not who you are. There wasn't even any light, just pure dark and silence. Then a voice, kind and caring. Suddenly I had something to define who I was. I knew this voice and it was not kind, and it was not caring, it was Lucifer, once an angel of God, and he wasn't here to help me. He was trying to settle the score, and this time I didn't have Sam to protect me. He laughed with glee at the prospect of sharpening his claws on this defenceless little mouse. I had nowhere to run, I couldn't hide. Slumped forward and lifeless, I was at his mercy.

Chapter Thirty-Two

He walked towards me like a hyena slowly circling its prey before pouncing to devour its victim. He was relishing this moment, as though the fear and helplessness of it all gave him some kind of sick pleasure and energy. From somewhere deep inside something awoke within me. It was anger, years of anger, and now it had a purpose.

"So what are you waiting for? Why don't you finish me off, you sadistic bastard?"

"Yes, I can imagine you would prefer that, but not so soon."

"You interest me, and believe me that doesn't happen very often."

"I thought you were all powerful, you could do whatever you wanted."

He flew into a rage. That I, a mere mortal at his mercy, should dare to question his power.

"Don't think to play with me you decrepit mortal. You call yourself human as though it means something special. I could squash you like a fly. Why do you all think you are so perfect? Do you really think God cares what happens to you? To me, you are just another piece of crap I wipe off my shoes. Sooner or later he is going to tire of you humans, with your insignificant religions and this thing you call faith. When was the last time you had faith? When did your faith ever save you? You only pray for help when you want something."

"So squash me then. Or are you just full of wind? Or is the all-powerful Lucifer afraid that God will stop him, because even Lucifer can be pitied."

He raised one hand and pointed to me. My body lifted into the air, my spine arched backwards, and at the same time I screamed in pain. It was as though searing hot pokers were being stabbed into my heart.

I thought my back would snap, and then he flung me to the floor. Through clenched teeth, and fighting back the pain, I managed to summon the strength to talk.

"Is that the best you can do you satanic bastard?"

Again he lifted a finger and pointed at me; at the same time the pain shot through me again.

"You have spirit but you are also very stupid. Do you think you can really keep doing this?"

Blood was dripping from my nose and mouth but I didn't care anymore. I had resigned myself to my fate and death was a welcome friend.

"So why don't you just finish me of? What's so special about me? Don't you have a war to start in some poverty-stricken country?"

"Very good, you have wit, but that's later on in my diary. I do love how easily you humans squabble over things. The hate you generate is truly magnificent."

Although he was mocking me I knew he was serious. Lucifer appeared to become more powerful the more I suffered. I was just one soul; imagine what a country fighting for some lost cause would do for him? It would be like hooking him up to the national power grid.

"You fascinate me. Do you know who your travelling companion is yet? Or is that still his little secret?"

I was in pain, I was lost, but I was dammed if he was going to have his little game with me.

"Don't tell me he's really the Archangel Gabriel and you're the big bad wolf? Or should that be Little Red Riding Hood?"

"So you don't know do you? How wonderful. The deceit is mind-numbingly simple and still you don't see it. Let me give you a clue, knucklehead. He's a Nazarene, though he wears his hair a little different these days, but then fashions change or so I am told.

He tried to save you pathetic people once, but all you did was crucify him. I could have saved him a lot of bother and told him that's what you would do but, no, he went ahead and did it all the same.

"I even offered him an entire kingdom if he would join me, but he just mumbled something about not tempting the Lord your God. He didn't get it, he's not my God, and thousands have taken me up on my offer since, and they didn't even have to be crucified. In fact, why carry on with all this? It doesn't have to be this way. Just say you will bow down to me and I will give you everything you could wish for. It's all so simple. Imagine, no mortgage, membership to an exclusive club and never having to worry about anything again. You know it makes sense. After all, I am going to win in the end."

"Yeah right, and you expect me to believe you, the father of all lies, the Antichrist. Your heart is so poisoned you would sell your mother if you had one. In fact, if you had a mother maybe you would understand that love and faith is the very reason why you will never win. I pity you, all that power and yet you are powerless to have the one thing you can never have, the love that a God gives his son."

"Oh I am so sad. Yes, please save me. You're pathetic, but you will not bate me, and save your pity for someone who cares. You are right I am the Antichrist, as you so astutely observed. So you see that kind of makes your saviour and travelling companion my opposite number, the Christ Jesus himself. How plain does it have to be?"

His words were twisted. He was the Antichrist and he was evil, but as twisted as he was I knew in that moment he was telling the truth.

The father of the greatest lie was, maybe for the first time in his life, telling the truth. Then why me? I had been asking this question from the start. What was so special about me? Why didn't Sam just tell me? OK, I might not have believed him at first, after all it took me a while to believe I was in heaven. The boat, the fishermen, my mind was swirling around. This meant the fisherman was Peter, not just any Peter, but The Peter. And Elizabeth and Simon, the jigsaw crashed into place. Still there was a missing piece, why? I had spent most of my life denying God. Surely someone like Mother Teresa would have been more worthy of such a blessing. I was just a simple man, and yet Jesus himself was my guide. Had he made a mistake? No, God didn't make mistakes, but then again here I was being tortured by Lucifer. Was this a case of mistaken identity? After all, there are a lot of souls crossing into heaven; mistakes are bound to be made.

Lucifer was still circling me like a vulture, waiting for that moment for me to give up my last breath.

"So the question I guess you are still asking is, 'Why you?' And there, my pathetic friend, I am afraid to say, I, too, would like to know why. Usually you are met by departed loved ones. Actually, that's not true. Some find their way to me, but those that find my place a little hot don't usually get the V.I.P. escorted reception. And, when we first met, the Nazarene was very cagey, almost as if he had something to hide. Then again, he's meant to be the pure one so that doesn't really fit. So what is it about you he doesn't want me to know?"

I had no idea where this was going. I was just an ordinary man.

I had done nothing special in my life, no major mountains climbed and no Nobel prizes. So I was just as much in the dark as Lucifer, and he knew it.

He continued to circle me, but I didn't care. I was beyond caring now. Just to breathe was an effort, and every part of me was wracked with pain.

Chapter Thirty-Three

At first it didn't register, but slowly I became aware of a pinprick of light on the ground in front of me. I thought it was my mind playing tricks. Maybe it was from the battering Lucifer had just given me.
My blood was still dripping on the floor from the assortment of cuts to my face. The light started getting brighter and brighter, and it took all the effort and strength I had to lift my head up and open my eyes. The room, if you could call this place a room, was getting brighter as well. Lucifer started backing into the shadows and I could see that his face was gnarled in anger.
"No, you can't do this to me! This is my dominion!" he shouted. "You know the rules, you get the good ones, I get the bad ones!"
Then came a voice, familiar and comforting. It was Sam or, now as I knew, Jesus.
"Lucifer. God does not live by your rules. You are the father of all lies, you enter God's house and yet expect me to stay away from yours.
"This soul belongs to God, and you shall not tempt the Lord your God."
"He is not my God, Nazarene, and he never will be. Since the first war in heaven I swore I would never again humble myself to him."
"One day all will stand and humble themselves before God, even you Lucifer. As your heart is filled with hate, God's heart is filled with love."
"Never, and I will crush this pathetic soul that lies at my feet. Call it my sacrificial offer to you."
Jesus lifted up his hand and there was an intense light, but it did not hurt my eyes. Lucifer cowered and cringed as though the light

was burning him. Still protesting, he lunged towards me, but he was thrown back into the air and crashed to the ground. He pounded his fists into the ground and the floor shook.

"He is mine, Nazarene, and I will have him!"

But his words were powerless against the light, and my body once again rose into the air. This time I was filled with immense peace and love, as I began to float upwards towards Jesus. It all started to feel like a dream, parts of the jigsaw puzzle were fitting into place, but still the major parts, the bits that confirmed my sanity, were missing.

From the pit below, which was now dark again, came a voice like a spoilt child who had just had his toy taken away from him.

"I will crush your pathetic people. How can you love such weakness? They still cling onto money and go to war in your name. Nothing has changed since you walked the earth. Don't you get it? Bit by bit I am winning this war, and then you will lie before me and beg for mercy."

But Jesus did not answer; he just smiled and continued to lift me up into his arms.

Chapter Thirty-Four

Once again we were in heaven, and the sky was the most radiant blue I had ever seen. Jesus touched me on the head and the pain left my body. Tears began to fill my eyes.

"Why didn't you tell me, Lord, who you were? I feel ashamed that I treated you like a normal man. You are the Son of God."

"That is why I did not tell you. You would have treated me differently, just as they did in Jerusalem and Nazareth. Remember, prophets are never accepted in their own land. You needed to be able to be yourself to take this journey, and if I told you who I was we would have had little conversation and, don't you agree, that might have been a bit boring. People feel they are beyond saving. They think that I would not talk to them because they are sinners. How quickly people forget you are all God's people. I came to save the sinners, not the righteous. The times may have changed, but the message is still the same. Lucifer wants you to forget who you are. His biggest trick is to first convince you he does not exist, and then to convince you God does not exist. A thousand years is but a day to God, and his love for you is without limits. All will one day return into balance."

I was with Christ. Me, actually with Christ. So many questions and yet I could think of nothing to ask. I felt unclean, unworthy of this honour. What had I done to deserve so much attention?

"You see, already you treat me differently. I am still your friend, Alex, still that same guy you called Sam."

"But, master, you are not the same. You are the Son of God. You were crucified and died for us. How can I just go back to arguing and talking to you like some guy on the street corner?"

"It is this attitude that separates you from me, and it is this that keeps you away from God. This is what Lucifer loves because then he can tempt you, bribe you, and turn you. I ate with my disciples, lived among them and came to earth to show them the way back home. Though they looked to me as the Messiah, I was also their brother and companion. Why do you think you are less than them? "We all play a part in this story. Your part is to find out who you are and what part you have played. When you do this, you will be free."

"But, master, we can't all be great."

"In God's eyes you are all great. The farmer who tends the land, the pop star, the taxi driver, you all are God's people. No one is greater or lesser than the other. I once tried to tell you this when I compared you to the lilies of the valley, and how God looks after even the smallest of creatures, and are you not greater than theses creatures? "You think you are so lost that God no longer wants to find you. A farmer may have a whole flock of sheep but, if one goes missing, do you think he will not spend the whole day looking for it? And when he finds that one simple sheep he is overjoyed. It does not mean he loves the others less; it's just that he knows they are safe and he does not need to worry about them. So don't put yourself down, Alex. If you feel distant from me, it is not because I am any different from the travelling companion you call Sam, it is because you have moved away from me."

Then he gave me a bear hug that almost winded me. "My brother," he said, "you have returned home and I have missed you."

Chapter Thirty-Five

I was in the presence of Christ and I felt so unworthy of this honour. After all, what do you say to the Son of God? For some strange reason all I wanted to do was cry. I had a feeling that this would somehow cleanse my soul. It was the comfort one seeks from a parent, in the knowledge and reassurance that everything is going to be OK. I felt relaxed and at peace, a peace I had never felt before, and my body felt limp as though I was floating on air.

"This is the final step in your journey. Let it be a bold step, Alex. It is said when the student is ready the master will appear. You are that student, Alex, and here is the twist. The master is within you, and all you have to do is find him. So many people search externally for the truth, some even take a lifetime to find it, and some never find it.

But the truth is often closer than you think. Have you ever looked for something and not seen it, because you had a preconceived idea of what it looked like and where it was? This is what happens when people search for themselves. They are looking for the light to go on that one perfect answer to their true spiritual self.

"They search so hard that they don't see the perfect light shining from within."

I knew what Jesus meant. All those times we rush this way and that in search of something, but we don't stop to see the sunrise and the wonder of the world around us. Then, when it's too late, our life is over, and only then we look back can we see what was really important. It was not the fast car or the big house; it was the people and friends that cared about us. The times we laughed, the times we held our children's hands, and all the simple things that were free and God given.

"Master, you suffered great pain for us. Why did you not just raise your hand and set yourself free? After all, we are still killing each other, and there is still hate in the world, and we still sin."

"Let me answer that by telling you about prayer. I used to love telling stories, you call them parables. In that period in physical form on earth with the disciples, not many people were educated, so not many people could read or write. This is why I told stories that made people think, and to this day even those who do not go to church still remember these stories from childhood. In parts of the world today, where the people are poor and still not educated, this tradition still carries on. For example, in parts of Africa when a child is named they recite the whole lineage of the child for generations back, all by memory and word of mouth. In the stories I told are hidden answers more simple than the story itself.

"A priest once visited one of his parishioners who was ill, and after comforting her he said, 'Would you mind if I pray for you?' She was happy for the priest to do this, as she was in great deal of pain at times.

Before he prayed he said to her, "What is it that you want God to do for you?"

What the woman said next surprised him, because when he asked this question in the past to others who were also suffering, be it mental anguish or physical pain, they all said, "Please ask God to take away this pain."

"All I want," she said, "is for God to give me the strength to get through the challenge of each day, because I accept that this is just life. We all get old. We all suffer in one way or another, but it is the humility with which we carry our burden that counts."

The priest looked at her and smiled. "My child," he said, "in saying this you already have the strength and humility you seek."

"So you see I, too, accepted that if I was to come into this world and be made flesh, I had to accept all that it was to be incarnate."

I had often wondered what it would be like to travel back in time and be with Christ. To ask him all those questions you never had answers to. Then as time passed I went out into the world and started

WHEN THE STUDENT IS READY THE MASTER WILL APPEAR

looking for my own answers. I found life hard, so I came to the conclusion that there was no God after all. I also decided that since scientists could not prove God's existence, I would accept that you live, you die and that's it. So being here in heaven, a place I did not believe in, then discovering that Lucifer and Christ were real as well, you would have thought I would be firing questions left, right and centre. No. Not one question. Nothing. In the moment of realization that Jesus was real, I felt a sense of peace as though I didn't need to have all those questions answered, as if I already knew the answers. It was like someone trying to figure out why it was so dark, and then someone throws a switch and suddenly it all makes sense. Of course, there was still one question I wanted an answer to. And I knew only I could find the answer to this. So who was I?

I though I was Alex, but who was Alex? I had a vague memory of my life on earth, children, a wife, even a job. I called myself Alex because that is what Jesus had called me, what the girl in the woods had called me. What was her name? I felt as though I was grasping for answers through a thin veil. If only I could just see through it.

Then I looked into his eyes and I knew I was the sanest person in the world. So why was it so difficult to know who I was? Why did Lucifer want me? Why had Jesus felt it necessary to greet me in person? Why not just send a loved one that had passed over? Lucifer was right, and in the answer to the question, I knew, was the answer to who I was.

Chapter Thirty-Six

I felt like a cup that was full and overflowing. The sudden realization about Jesus and his identity, and the fight with Lucifer; I had no more room inside me to take on any more information. At least, not of such epic proportions.

I sat down and, for a while, I was unable to say anything. All the time he stood by me also in silence.

"So tell me," I said, "what were the disciples really like? We have been told very little about them. We know about some of them and what they have to say about you, but not much about them as men."

"They were really no different from you. They were men from different backgrounds. Some with families, some without, but, essentially, normal men and women. All looking and searching for truth, struggling to get by in life.

"Hold on, I don't remember any women disciples."

"Who do you think looked after us? In those days women often travelled with the men. However, they were considered second-class citizens. Believe me, though, in God's eyes there was no inequality, and man's prejudice was not mine. If I was to return to the earth and once again take on physical form, in a world where women have become more equal, you would find I would have many female disciples."

"Why didn't any of them write about you then? I don't remember the gospel according to Martha."

"To have written about me could have been dangerous for them. Remember, in those days men made all the decisions, and held all the power. They would have felt threatened if a woman dared to rock their patriarchal throne. As I said before, there was also the fact that only the rich and powerful, who could afford education, could read and write. So also throw into this restrictive scenario being born a woman, and you can see why you don't hear about them."

"It's obvious when you put it like that but, just because they were with you, does that make them disciples?"

"All who follow me are disciples. All who want peace in the world are disciples. Being a disciple it not a privilege of power restricted to the few."

"I think this might shake a few people's foundations."

"That's not such a bad thing. Just as a butterfly needs to break free of the confines of its chrysalis in order to fly, so too must the human race shed prejudicial, archaic ideas in order to grow."

"So would you say they were radicals?"

"They didn't think much of the Romans, if that's what you mean. They also didn't like paying taxes. Beyond this though, they knew there had to be more meaning to the life they were living. Peter was a bit of a sceptic. At first he thought I was just another holy man making empty promises with hidden agendas. A bit like you and your humour, this is one of the qualities I like about him because he was not afraid to question."

"Did they also treat you differently when they found out who you were?"

"Yes, and some of them felt ashamed. Peter's self-torment at denying me was, at times, worse than the pain of crucifixion. My physical pain passed, but Peter's lasted longer. He felt he had betrayed the Messiah and a friend, but actually he had done what most people would have done when they are confused and scared."

"If I was around then I would never have betrayed you."

"You say that in hindsight based on what you now know."

I felt as though I was being judged. How could Jesus say this? Betrayal was something I detested. I had been betrayed once by someone who I thought was a good friend, only to find out he was two-faced. I remember how hurt I had felt. Then I remembered who I was talking to.

"Forgive me if I talk out of turn, Lord, but I would never betray you, and not just because you are Christ, but you have become a friend to me, and friends don't betray friends."

He looked straight at me and with those steel blue-grey eyes, just like the first time I had met him. I felt like they were looking into the depths of my soul. Except this time, because I now knew who he was, I also knew that's exactly what he was doing. I felt a little uncomfortable with this thought. How naive of me to think that Jesus could not see the truth in my soul. He knew me as I knew myself, maybe even better.

"Alex, like Peter, you also betrayed me but, unlike Peter, you have lived in purgatory ever since. Your hell has been self-persecution.

"My crucifixion was meant to set you free, not enslave you."

"What are you talking about?"

I was totally confused. How could I have betrayed him? Granted, since arriving in heaven, the longer I spent here the harder it was to remember my earth life, but betray him? Never. If anything, I had not believed in him, but that was not really betrayal.

"So I didn't believe in you, I didn't go to church, but you can't compare that to Peter's betrayal. He knew who you were, he was your disciple and friend, and, as for purgatory, that's a bit strong."

"Alex, before you came to heaven where were you?"

"In a wood, naked, alone and then scared."

"Don't you still wonder how you got there?"

"Yes, ever since I arrived here. Don't tell me you know? What am I talking about? Of course you know."

"Do you remember how I told you that your perception of heaven is based on what you think it should be? Just like light and dark, heaven and hell and purgatory, they are one and the same. All are based on your personal preconceived perception. That's why you will find so many accounts of purgatory. Not everyone will describe it like Dante's hell. Your purgatory was to be alone and lost in the middle of the woods. Being naked only compounds this as you are exposed to your core; you had nothing to hide behind."

"But I was only there for a short time; not much of a purgatory."

"Were you there for a short time? How do you know that?"
"Because I remember being tucked up in a warm bed just before that."
"Tell me, Alex, do you like the woods?"
"Yes, I love being in the woods."
"Then why were you so scared?"
I remember sitting outside the log cabin and, fleetingly, I thought about being scared, but I remember once I was clothed and warm I felt safe again. Jesus was right, why had I been so scared?
"I don't know. It was strange. As a child I would play for hours in the woods without a care in the world."
"The reason you were scared was you took a place that you loved and intentionally turned it into a place you were scared of. This way it became your purgatory. You felt so bad about betraying me that you started destroying everything that was meaningful to you. What was once good became bad, and what was bad became good."
"I don't buy that. It didn't last long enough. Noisulli found me shortly after I woke up. So how could my betrayal have been that bad? Otherwise I would still be there."
"And if you relived that one moment when you woke up naked and alone, and then felt absolute fear over and over again, would that have made your hell more real for you?"
"Are you saying that is what happened?"
"Yes."
I felt sick. It was like passing an accident you don't want to look at, but something compels you turn your head and face the trauma.
My mind was so confused; it was swimming with question after question. I knew he was right. This was the Son of God, and he was making me face the depths of my soul. A place I did not want to go to, but was being drawn to like a moth to a flame. "No," I kept saying to myself, this couldn't be true. Why would I persecute my self so much?
I thought martyrs were self-pitying fools. All they did was hurt people in meaningless statements of self-destruction. They tell us they are trying to make a statement about the sanctity of life, and yet in taking their own do the exact opposite.

Then I thought about our conversations about time.

"So was it a week, or even a month?"

"You are right. It's not long, but try over two thousand years."

"What!"

I was pacing backwards and forwards now. I could feel the anger welling up inside me.

"What in the hell would I do that for? That's just bloody stupid! What changed then? How did I get here? Why am I not still there in the woods beating up on my self?"

"Because, after all that time, one day you did something different, you got down on your knees and called me. Did you think it was a coincidence that Noisulli should appear at that exact moment?

"Do you remember thinking that she looked like she was floating along in front of you, and how you dismissed it, because you thought it was your imagination playing tricks on you in all the confusion?"

I thought back to when I first saw her. She was the most beautiful woman I had ever seen.

"Are you telling me she has something to do with you?"

"All I can say, Alex, is be aware angels walk amongst you."

"You sent an angel to get me. Why did she have to be so beautiful? Why could you not have sent a man?"

"Would you have followed a man so easily? You were scared enough as it was. I think being confronted by a strange man while also being naked would have sent you in the opposite direction."

"So the log cabin, the horse, all more projections of my thoughts?"

"Yes, even the accident at the stream. I had to ease you into this slowly. Sorry about the pain in your ribs but, if it's any consolation, that was not real either. I had to bring you here slowly so you could find out who you are. And when you called to me I answered. You don't know how long I have been waiting for you to do that."

"And all because you say I betrayed you."

"No, all because you think you betrayed me. There is a big difference."

Then I was uncomfortable, very uncomfortable. The jigsaw, the missing piece, was falling into place.

WHEN THE STUDENT IS READY THE MASTER WILL APPEAR

"Hold on, back up here. You said I have been in self-imposed purgatory for over two thousand years. And all this time you have been waiting for me. That means I betrayed you over two thousand years ago. Which means I was there when you were crucified, and I was there when Peter denied you. The only other person whose betrayal was greater than Peter's was...

"No, it's not possible, not me, I wouldn't do that! Please, Lord, tell me it's not true."

My legs gave way and I fell to my knees, and then I threw up. Tears filled my eyes. I sobbed like a wounded child. I cried and screamed as though two thousand years of pain was being spilled to the ground. My chest was heaving, grasping for air, seeking for some other explanation. I was finding it harder and harder to breath, but I knew there was only one answer.

I felt a hand on my shoulder. He lifted me to my feet and held me in his arms.

"Yes, Judas my brother, the lost lamb has returned to the father, and his heart cries with joy."

"But, Lord, I betrayed you."

"No, Judas, you did not. I had to be crucified. I even asked God to lift the burden from me if it was possible. I knew that I had been sent for man's salvation, and that you had been sent to be a part of that.

"Too long the world has portrayed you as the betrayer. Your kiss was that of a friend not an enemy. It is time to forgive yourself and come home."

The light filled my body and my body was no more. Then the light filled my soul and I was at peace.

Chapter Thirty-Seven

Though my eyes were closed I was still aware of the light and the musty smell, which somehow felt out of place. There was a sensation as though I was gently rocking backwards and forwards like a child in my mother's arms. I wanted to wake up but at the same time was happy to feel safe and comforted. In the distance I became aware once again of a familiar voice that began to permeate my conscious. With my eyes closed I strained to make it out. I could hear my name but it felt far away and muffled, as though someone was trying to talk to me through a door.

"Alex. You are safe and protected, calm and relaxed."

Safe from what? Why should I feel I need to be protected? I was with Christ. If I was not safe with him I would never be safe. I had discovered who I was, I had battled with Lucifer, and still Christ loved me. I betrayed him, I was responsible for his crucifixion and still he loved me. He had released me from my bond, from a self-imposed hell. So why did I need protecting?

"With each breath in and each breath out, Alex, you feel yourself coming round."

I didn't want to come back into my body. I was happy to stay with my master. I no longer cared about the physical body, and all I wanted now was to stay with him and be at peace.

"Slowly feel yourself coming back, Alex."

"No, I don't want to come back." I felt as though I was sinking now, and the feeling of being light was being replaced by a heavy sensation, as though each molecule of my body was solidifying.

"Five, four, three, two, one, eyes slowly open and come round."

I was back in the office, and it took a while for my surroundings to become familiar.

WHEN THE STUDENT IS READY THE MASTER WILL APPEAR

"Alex, how do you feel?"

"Not sure, really. It all felt so real. Where did that all come from? I don't even go to church."

"The subconscious is a wonderful thing. We don't always understand it and, I have to say in all my years in practice, I have never experienced such a graphic hypnosis session. You might find that over the next few day things will become clear to you. I wouldn't worry about it, though"

"But it was all so real, doc. I could smell and feel everything. It felt as though I was actually there."

"The mind is a powerful thing, and what you think is real is often not. Things sometimes end up back to front so what is real becomes unreal, and what is unreal becomes real."

"I don't get it. Everything was very real, nothing was back to front."

"That's what I mean, Alex. Do you remember that girl's name?"

"How could I forget her? If only I could find a woman like that. Her name was Noisulli. She was so real, doc, I could even smell her."

"Was she, Alex? Did you ever wonder why she was so perfect? When you look into a mirror things are reversed."

He wrote something down on his pad and handed it to me.

"Here, take this to the mirror over there and hold it up."

I had no idea what he was talking about. It felt like some sort of parlour game. Nevertheless, I decided to go along with it. So I took the pad and walked to the mirror. I held up the pad and read what was written on the notepad. Illusion.

"Now read the notepad, Alex."

"Noisulli." How could I have not seen it?

"I don't get it. That's freaky. Why would I come up with that?"

"Only you have the answer to that, Alex. Maybe she is the woman you would like to be with, your idea of the perfect woman. We all imagine our perfect partner, but usually it's just an illusion.

"No one is truly perfect. Often the most perfect person is a reflection of ourselves. Remember, you came here to find out why you keep attracting the same type of woman into your life. You told me there must be something you had to learn."

I don't know if I found out anything about my relationships, but I did have a profound sense that I had discovered something important about myself. And in that moment I swear that if I had closed my eyes I would be back with him.

I paid the doctor and left his practice feeling confused, but at the same time at peace and content. The sun was warm and comforting and all around me people went about their busy lives. I crossed the road and walked up the steep steps. The doors were made of solid oak and I reached out and pulled the handle towards me, and the heavy doors opened. And then I did something I had not done since childhood, I went into the church.

THE END

Printed in the United Kingdom
by Lightning Source UK Ltd.
116505UKS00001B/100-108